A QUAKER PRAYER LIFE

David Johnson

Inner Light Books
San Francisco, California
2013

A Quaker Prayer Life

© David Johnson, 2013

All Rights Reserved

Cover and book design: Charles Martin

Published by Inner Light Books, San Francisco, California

www.innerlightbooks.com

editor@innerlightbooks.com

Library of Congress Control Number: 2013947319

ISBN 978-0-9834980-5-6 (hardcover)
ISBN 978-0-9834980-6-3 (paperback)
ISBN 978-0-9834980-7-0 (eBook)

Introduction

Prayer is a conscious choice to seek God, in whatever form that Divine Presence speaks to each of us, moment to moment. The difficulties we experience in inward prayer are preparation for our outward lives. Each time we return to the centre in prayer we are modelling how to live our lives; each time we dismiss the internal intrusions we are strengthening that of God within us and denying the role of the Self; every time we turn to prayer and to God we are seeking an increase in the measure of Light in our lives.

A Quaker prayer life arises from a life of continuing daily attentiveness. The first generation of Quakers followed a covenant with God, based on assiduous obedience to the promptings of the Inward Light. This process did not require established churches, priests or liturgies. Quaker prayer then became a practice of patient waiting in silence.

Prayer is something to be done daily all through our lives, and not to be left till we go to Meeting for Worship once a week. Yet prayer is not easy for many of us. If you have ever felt the need to spend more time in prayer, but have pushed the leading aside because there is so much to be done before you get out of the house each day for work, read on. If you have ever felt troubled by the little time you devote to spiritual practice during your week, read on. If you have ever found yourself stressed and uncentred in your job wishing it were otherwise and that you were calmer and more in control, read on.

This essay has preserved the original wording of early Friends' writings except where quotes taken from recent anthologies have been modernized. The scriptural quotes are from the Authorised (King James) Version, except where noted. Both Quaker and biblical quotes have masculine language and a seventeenth-century cultural context that can seem strange to us. I hope readers can "translate" into their own words while seeking to understand the spiritual reality that underlies the original words.

Early Quaker Prayer Life

There are many forms of prayer. What is Quaker prayer? The early Quakers were very gifted in prayer; this can be seen in their perceptive writings, in the extraordinary inward power of their lives, and in the influence they had on others. Signs of this gift were described in William Penn's appreciation of George Fox, in the Preface to the original 1694 edition of Fox's Journal:

> *But above all he excelled in prayer. The inwardness and weight of his spirit, the reverence and solemnity of his address and behaviour, and the fewness and fullness of his words, have often struck even strangers with admiration, as they used to reach others with consolation. The most awful [Full of Awe], reverent frame I ever beheld, I must say, was his in prayer.*[1]

Early Friends did not leave a manual on prayer for us to follow. However there is enough advice scattered in their writings to make clear much of their practice. The different emphases in each of the writings may reflect an individual's calling, for the Spirit does guide us to pray in different ways along the journey. The differences may also reflect that the writing was done to draw attention to some aspect in the spiritual life that the writer had just immediately noticed, and so was instructed to comment upon. None of the individual writings thus imply that any specific advice given is "all there is to it".

Many of the early Quaker writings were published to express a practical, personal experience rather than give a theoretical explanation, and so exhort seekers to try this form of prayer for themselves.

George Fox's advices for prayer and advancing the spiritual life were to live in the Light, mind that which is pure within you, love the Light no matter what it shows you, and accept Jesus' teachings. In times of trouble, his advice was to look neither to the right nor the left, that is stay centred, and to look over corruptions to the Light.

Similar advice is given in the Cloud of Unknowing (ca.1370) regarding intrusive memories or thoughts:

> *[Y]ou are resolutely to step over them, because of your deep love for God; you must trample them down underfoot..., try to look, as it were, over their shoulders, seeking something else—which is God, shrouded in the cloud of unknowing.*[2]

Some may say nowadays that there is no such thing as Quaker prayer, for Friends encompass a very wide range of spiritual attitudes and beliefs, and draw on spiritual writings and images from many sources. Certainly there are also remarkable similarities between the ethical stances of all religions and in the practices of meditation and prayer. We can learn and be guided in many ways.

However, I choose to persist in trying to understand and practise closely what the first generation of Quakers discovered. I seek to understand and implement the advices for prayer given by those earlier Quakers, so many of whom led inspired lives.

The term 'God' and the words 'Kingdom of God' have proved very difficult for some, carrying the associations of unhelpful doctrines and limitations of meaning, especially with the authoritarian masculine images. However I have used this word because it is widespread in early writings, and quote it as used in the original documents. I am sure the early Quakers had a much broader concept of God than has been taught in some modern churches. The *Early Quakers and 'The Kingdom of God'* (2012) by Gerard Guiton provides a detailed account of this topic.[3]

'God', for me, is simply a three-letter word that refers to that extraordinary inner mystery of Divine Presence in all its manifestations: creating, sustaining, enlightening, pacifying, reproving, guiding, inspiring and energising. It carries no theological doctrine or ritual requirements. It is simply a short word to convey that huge range of inward mystical feelings and understandings, most of which cannot be put into words. Many words have been used to refer to this mystery by others, most of them longer: Universal Wisdom, Divine Presence, Eternal Presence, Supreme End, Infinite Light, Love, Truth, Creator, the NeverChanging, the Infinite, Immutable, OmniPresent One, Un-nameable, Source of all Being, All that has been that is and ever will be, That in which I live and move and have my being, Great Spirit, etc. I use the three letters 'G', 'o', 'd'. To enter into the Kingdom of God is to enter into a state, in the present, of deep awareness, connectedness and responsiveness to the divine implantings of Truth and Love, so we can do no other.

Prayer is for me an act of total turning of my being toward God, that Divine Presence, and of surrendering to it.

Covenant of Light

The first generation of Quakers engaged in prayer in a radically different way than the established churches. The religious life in churches was based on liturgies led by priests or similar officiants, with expectation of attendance at church, the payment of tithes and other parish work; and these practices were not only part of the social framework but were also implied as necessary for personal salvation. The monarchical government reinforced and provided legal sanctions to support these beliefs.

The early Quakers separated from the established Churches to practise a radically different pattern of prayer and life. One way to view the new direction of the Quakers is to consider the series of covenants established between God and people:[4]

Covenant of Works—People are to follow God's laws, as written in the Pentateuch, with the main laws codified as The Ten Commandments, so that their lives and work lead to the protection of God and to personal salvation. The history of the ancient Hebrews shows a people who at times follow God's laws and receive blessings, and at other times stray wildly and are then subjected to wars and misery. This punishment model does not sit well with many people today.

Covenant of Grace—People are given God's grace for faith and for their works, a faith received through the pulpit from ordained ministers of a nationally accepted church, and a resulting grace which enables them to handle the ups and downs of living in the world. The Puritans considered Scripture could form the basis for a new Godly system of government and national behaviour, though violence was acceptable in establishing this new order.

Covenant of Light—People receive grace for obedience to the promptings and directions of the Inward Light. All self-justification is to be overcome so that the Light becomes the driving force of life. No churches and ordained ministers are required, though a strong and faithful obedience to the Inward Light is paramount. Violence is unacceptable. Though the Bible remained a justification for the first Quakers, the prime inspiration was direct experience of the Holy Spirit and a realisation that indeed Jesus, as the Eternal Christ, had come again to teach people himself.

'Christ' is the Greek word for the anointed one. The Greek transliteration of ancient Hebrew or Aramaic words in the original gospel manuscripts was 'Messiah'.[5] Both words mean the same thing. The term is often applied exclusively to Jesus; however it is an ancient wisdom. Many of us will also have experienced it in some small way—an experience of divine presence that is like being gently touched, perhaps with a finger dipped in warm fragrant oil, and we feel that warmth and special inward touch, and in that moment are momentarily aware of some deep religious understanding, or of a purifying presence. That is to say, we have been anointed, and it is a sign we have been in the eternal presence — we have known the Eternal Christ within us:

> *But the anointing which ye have received of him abideth in you, and ye need not that any man teach you: but as the same anointing teacheth you of all things, and is truth, and is no lie, and even as it hath taught you, ye shall abide in him. (1 John 2:27)*

This early Christian experience and teaching that an inward anointing abides within each of us was attested by George Fox and by the early Quaker Elizabeth Bathurst:

> *But I brought them the Scriptures, and told them there was an anointing within man to teach him, and the Lord would teach them himself.*[6]

> *For 'tis that Spiritual Anointing that the Apostle John speaks of, which those that have received it (and in whom it abides) needs not that any Man teach them, but as the same Anointing teacheth them all things....*[7]

Quaker prayer then became an effort to discern this Inward Light and its requirements. Such prayer demanded transcendence beyond normal thoughts and words, and an attitude of humble surrender to the Light. Early Friends were well aware that this transformation could only be effected with the help of God; that in fact God prepares our hearts to enable true prayer. The result of surrendering to God was the instilling of wonderful wisdom, and a life and power and courage that went beyond normal abilities. The strength to suffer patiently without resorting to violence for their faith became a hallmark of early Quakers.

The Practical Background for Quaker Prayer

Many of us have read extracts of the Quaker saints and thought how much we would like to lead a life like that—so centred, so inspired, so courageous, so productive. Those people did not lead such lives just by working hard and going to Meeting for Worship once a week, perhaps missing meeting if there was too much going on.

If we delve into the stories of those people's lives we find that their spiritual life was central, and was practised every day. Scripture was read daily. Meeting for Worship was generally attended twice a week. They practised their spiritual work first and foremost, and took their spirituality with them everywhere they went. They took Jesus' advice seriously: "Seek ye *first* the kingdom of God and all else will be added unto you". (Matthew 6:33; Luke 12:31 emphasis added)

Consider the family life of William and Gulielma Penn:

> *In summer they rose at five, in winter at seven, in spring and autumn at six; a real daylight-saving arrangement. They had breakfast at nine, dinner at twelve, supper at seven and to bed at ten. They assembled with the servants for worship in the morning; and at eleven to make a recess in the work of the forenoon they met again for reading the Bible and other religious books. At six in the evening, the servants reported on what they had done, and received orders for the next day. 'Loud discourses and troublesome noise' were forbidden. All quarrels were to be made up before bedtime.*[8]

The early Quaker and strenuous communicator, one of the First Publishers of Truth, Edward Burrough, described some of their early meetings for worship:

> *We met together often and waited upon the Lord in pure silence, from our own words and all men's*

words, and hearkened to the voice of the Lord, and felt His word in our hearts to burn up and beat down all that was contrary to God; and we obeyed the Light of Christ in us... and took up the cross to all earthly glories, crowns and ways, and denied ourselves, our relations and all that stood in the way betwixt us and the Lord. ...And while waiting upon the Lord in silence, as we often did for many hours together,... we received often the pouring down of the Spirit upon us ...and our hearts were made glad, and our tongues loosed, and our mouths opened...[9]

Some time before Elizabeth Fry died in 1845, she said to one of her daughters:

My dear, I can say one thing—since my heart was touched at the age of seventeen, I believe I have never awakened from sleep in sickness or health, by day or by night, without my first waking thought being how best I might serve the Lord.[10]

Stephen Grellet, the man who brought Elizabeth into her work in prisons had this to say, his words reflecting a practice, not of coming to the Spirit in prayer when it suited, but of abiding in that state permanently:[11]

Lie low, O my soul! Abide in humility and meekness before the Lord thy Redeemer, whom thou hast so frequently known to be thy Strength in weakness, thy Leader and deliverer.

In 1855 as he died, he cried out:

My heart and my strength faileth, but God is the strength of my heart and my portion for ever.

Nor should we think that daily prayer was only for those 'olden day' Friends; the reliance on daily retirement and prayer has been a regular practice for many throughout the last

360 years and still is for many today: *"and by [1936] ...,*
Bayard [Rustin] was, in Quaker fashion, 'depending upon my
daily periods for guidance'".[12]

The early Friends writings are replete with references to the
Bible. They were completely reliant on it as a source of
spiritual advice, example and nourishment. Modern liberal
unprogrammed Friends are commonly reluctant to read and
meditate upon the scriptures, let alone place their trust in
them. Early Friends were quite clear that Jesus, his teachings
and example, and also much of the Old Testament writings
were fundamental to their faith and practice.

We may think that if we read enough good books we will
come to know all about the spiritual life. Yet experience tells
us that after some years we may be painfully aware of the
limited spiritual progress we have made. Why is that? If our
knowledge is "head" knowledge it helps us learn about God,
but cannot take us towards God. The *Cloud of Unknowing*,
written in the early 1300s, makes a clear distinction that is
sometimes difficult for us moderns to enter into, for with our
extensive education we have difficulty believing that the mind
cannot solve everything:

> *All rational beings, angels and men, possess two*
> *faculties, the power of knowing and the power of*
> *loving. To the first, to the intellect, God who made*
> *them is forever unknowable, but to the second, to*
> *love, God is completely knowable, and that by every*
> *separate individual.*[13]

Thomas Kelly's advice was that the centred life comes with
practice, for this journey with the Spirit requires personal
surrender, great openness and, like all relationships, is built on
love and attention.

> *Down beneath the fluctuating change of heavenly*
> *elation and hellish discouragement we can carry on*
> *a well nigh continuous prayer life of submission,*

> *'Father into thy hands I commend my Spirit.' This*
> *internal prayer of submission of will we can carry*
> *on in the very midst of our busiest days. There is a*
> *way of carrying on our mental life at two levels at*
> *once, but it only comes with practice. At one level of*
> *our mental life we can be talking with people,*
> *dealing with problems, carrying the burdens that*
> *our calling in time puts upon us. But beneath all this*
> *occupation with time we can be in prayerful relation*
> *with the Eternal Goodness, quietly, serenely, joyfully*
> *surrendering ourselves and all that we are to Him.*[14]

The examples of solitary prayer set by Jesus, George Fox,
Gandhi, Bayard Rustin, Henri Nouwen and many others make
it clear that daily personal prayer is an essential part of the
spiritual journey—the willingness and then the delight in
spending time alone with God. As was noted of Jesus: " *And*
in the morning, rising up a great while before day, he went
out, and departed into a solitary place, and there prayed"
(Mark 1:35).[15] For some this is the prime spiritual practice,
though the group worship in meeting adds another dimension,
comfort and strength to a life of prayer.

All this reminds me of Paul's advice *"Pray without*
ceasing".[16] But how?

Step One: In Practice, Centre Down, "Turn thy Mind to the Light", and "Stand Still in the Light"

The traditional Quaker method was to centre down; 'center
down' is a term picked up by many others seeking progress in
meditation and prayer. As Elizabeth Bathurst noted in 1679
"*This effectual Operation of the Spirit ... cannot be known*
without a being centred down into the same:"[17] This advice
has two words, 'centre' and 'down', and we can examine each
in turn. Helen Gould in her Backhouse Lecture, an invited
annual presentation to Australia Yearly Meeting, has given a
very clear set of guidelines.[18] In the appendix are listed some
other ways people have found helpful to still the mind.

First the advice is to Centre

To "centre" is to constrain our inner attention to the central line within ourselves. In practice you may find it helpful to close your eyes and take three, measured, deep breaths to focus your attention internally, and during this to breathe a prayer that God will be present, and come to your assistance. The awareness can then be drawn in from each side, right and left, towards the centre. Commonly our attention is still extending forwards, as if the eyes are seeking something through the closed eyelids. The attention needs to be re-directed gently inwards until all our attention is directed inwards. There we wait patiently and attentively, dismissing any expectation of what will happen.

Whenever our mind wanders and we find ourselves having an internal discussion or observation about another person, a problem or a delight, we will find that our attention has been lured away from our inner space, typically somewhat off to one side, the right or the left. Noting this, we can gradually withdraw our inner attention back towards the centre. Do not become upset by these diversions. Brother Lawrence, also writing in the 1600s, found that:

> *I worshipped Him the oftenest that I could, keeping my mind in His holy presence, and recalling it as often as I found it wandered from Him. I found no small pain in this exercise, and yet I continued with it, notwithstanding all the difficulties that occurred, without troubling or disquieting myself when my mind wandered involuntarily.*[19]

The advice of Alexander Parker and then of Fox is to stay centred:

> *The first that enters into the place of your meeting, be not careless, nor wander up and down either in body or mind, but innocently sit down in some place and turn thy mind to the Light, and wait upon God*

singly, as if none were present but the Lord, and here thou are strong...[20]

Keep within. And when they shall say, 'lo here' or 'lo there is Christ', go not forth, for Christ is within you. And there are seducers and antichrists which draw your minds out from the teaching within you. For the measure is within, and the light of God is within, and the pearl is within you, which is hid; and the word of God is within you, and ye are the temples of God;...[21]

This second text draws on Luke 17: 20-21:

And when he was demanded of the Pharisees, when the kingdom of God should come, he answered them and said, The kingdom of God cometh not with observation: neither shall they say, Lo here! or lo there! for, behold the kingdom of God is within you.

Despite the common impression that the Old Testament reveals a God of external laws and judgements, the prophets are clear that divine commandments and guidance are also in our own hearts. No doubt Moses and the other prophets laid down the external laws as a ready reference, however the important guide is the inward voice in the heart:

For this commandment which I command thee this day, it is not hidden from thee, neither is it far off. It is not in heaven, that thou shouldest say, Who shall go up for us to heaven, and bring it unto us, that we may hear it, and do it? Neither is it beyond the sea, that thou shouldest say, Who shall go over the sea for us, and bring it unto us, that we may hear it, and do it? But the word is very nigh unto thee, in thy mouth, and in thy heart, that thou mayest do it.
(Deuteronomy 30:11-14)

And Samuel said, Hath the LORD as great delight in burnt offerings and sacrifices, as in obeying the voice of the LORD? Behold, to obey is better than sacrifice, and to hearken than the fat of rams. (1 Samuel 15:22)

I delight to do thy will, O my God: yea, thy law is within my heart. (Psalm 40:8)

Hearken unto me, ye that know righteousness, the people in whose heart is my law; fear ye not the reproach of men, neither be ye afraid of their revilings.

For the moth shall eat them up like a garment, and the worm shall eat them like wool: but my righteousness shall be for ever, and my salvation from generation to generation. (Isaiah 51:7-8)

Behold, the days come, saith the LORD, that I will make a new covenant with the house of Israel, and with the house of Judah: Not according to the covenant that I made with their fathers in the day that I took them by the hand to bring them out of the land of Egypt; which my covenant they brake, although I was an husband unto them, saith the LORD: But this shall be the covenant that I will make with the house of Israel; After those days, saith the LORD, I will put my law in their inward parts, and write it in their hearts; and will be their God, and they shall be my people. And they shall teach no more every man his neighbour, and every man his brother, saying, Know the LORD: for they shall all know me, from the least of them unto the greatest of them, saith the LORD: for I will forgive their iniquity, and I will remember their sin no more. (Jeremiah 31:31-34)

Then will I sprinkle clean water upon you, and ye shall be clean: from all your filthiness, and from all your idols, will I cleanse you. A new heart also will I give you, and a new spirit will I put within you: and I will take away the stony heart out of your flesh, and I will give you an heart of flesh. And I will put my spirit within you, and cause you to walk in my statutes, and ye shall keep my judgments, and do them. (Ezekiel 36:25-27)

And as re-stated by Jesus, Luke 17:20-21.

And when he was demanded of the Pharisees, when the kingdom of God should come, he answered them and said, The kingdom of God cometh not with observation: Neither shall they say, Lo here! or, lo there! for, behold, the kingdom of God is within you.

The message was not only to hear, but also to obey, to "do" what the divine prompting expected (Deuteronomy 30:11-14). The ancients were clear that God searches all hearts, and that this inward commandment is much more important than the letter of the external law.

And thou, Solomon my son, know thou the God of thy father, and serve him with a perfect heart and with a willing mind: for the LORD searcheth all hearts, and understandeth all the imaginations of the thoughts: if thou seek him, he will be found of thee; but if thou forsake him, he will cast thee off for ever. (1 Chronicles 28:9)

It is hard to overemphasise Jesus' words 'the Kingdom of God is within you' for they are probably the truest and most important advice on prayer Jesus ever gave. Do not look out in prayer through closed eyelids hoping to see something. We are to consciously and gently turn our attention inwards. The explanatory words from the title page of George Fox's 1658 statement on Quakerism, *The Pearle Found in England,* emphasise that the path is inward: *"the Pearl of God which is hid in all the World, that everyone may turn into himself, and then feel it and find it"*.[22]

An ancient advice on the same theme is in Proverbs (4:25-27):

> *Let thine eyes look right on, and let thine eyelids look straight before thee. Ponder the path of thy feet, and let all thy ways be established. Turn not to the right hand nor to the left: remove thy foot from evil.*

And in Isaiah (30:21):

> *And thine ears shall hear a word behind thee, saying, This is the way, walk ye in it, when ye turn to the right hand and when ye turn to the left.*

The same advice was mentioned even earlier by Joshua in his advices before dying, Joshua (23: 6), to the Israelites:

> *Be ye therefore very courageous to keep and do all that is written in the book of the law of Moses, that ye turn not aside therefrom to the right or to the left.*

Moses' instructions included both practical laws as well as inward attitudes. As Joshua emphasised Joshua (22:5):

> *But take diligent heed to do that commandment and the law, which Moses the servant of the Lord your God charged you, and to walk in all his ways, and to keep his commandments, and to cleave unto him, and to serve him with all your heart and with all your soul.*

The scripture texts are a warning on two levels. The first is not to be tempted by the external understandings proposed by many. For the disciples, apostles and followers of Jesus, they should concentrate on what Jesus has taught and not on the words of the Pharisees or other, later alternative teachings.

There is also an important deeper meaning. For in prayer the advice is: do not be tempted internally to allow your mind to wander, or be led by beguiling offers of imagined understandings in other thoughts or reasonings. Stay within, in the centre. The ears in Isaiah are our inward ears, listening patiently and attentively for the words of the Spirit.

Fox and the early Friends were totally committed to inward searching and revelation, and placed external preaching and reading as secondary guides. The most extraordinary thing about Fox as a spiritual teacher was he did not formulate a doctrinal framework but simply taught all to follow the inward guide. One story is that when William Penn admitted his discomfort on wearing a sword, Fox did not give specific policy advice, he simply said, "Wear it as long as thou canst" —that is, the inward guide will tell you what to do.

The Second Advice is Down

The motion of inner attention may be gently moved or followed downward, from the head to the heart, and can help sideline the insistent thoughts because they are at another place:

> *Therefore come down, come down into the Word of his patience, which is nigh in your hearts, which if you do, he will keep you in the hour of temptation...*[23]

We do not force the pace, and allow it to happen naturally. Isaac Penington uses the words "*sink down to the seed which God sows in the heart*":

> *Give over thine own willing, give over thy own running, give over thine own desiring to know or be anything and sink down to the seed which God sows in the heart, and let that grow in thee and be in thee and breathe in thee and act in thee; and thou shalt*

find by sweet experience that the Lord knows that and loves and owns that, and will lead it to the inheritance of Life, which is its portion.[24]

The Quaker practice to centre down is to withdraw our attention from the outside world, and then inwardly to confine our attention to the centre, and then gradually to allow it to sink down to the heart. We can do this in complete trust, for the Spirit will lead and prompt us. Penington has also used the term 'breathe in thee', and many have found that some care following the pattern of breathing within can lead to deeper places and openings.

However there is no need to force any particular movement to "happen". Sometimes it is quite sufficient to maintain a simple awareness, or to respond to the stirrings of grace by uplifting the heart in thankfulness and adoration to God. It is most important to determinedly stay away from ANY thoughts, and to want to happen what God wants to happen. On finishing a meditation and prayer, it is important we give thanks, and then try to rise calmly and carry the presence and stillness in our heart.

It is good to practise this method often, and initially an extended period such as a retreat for a weekend may be helpful to find the way in. If this is not possible, then 2-3 hours in patient practice can help. Or, 10-30 minutes each day, perhaps at morning on rising is a good start.

When we have experienced a time of enlightened prayer, when the Spirit has spoken strongly and perhaps melted part of our resistance to God, it is very important to follow that with one or two periods of prayer within a few hours and certainly within a day. Otherwise it is all too easy for each of us to begin to feel we can take some credit for the process. Not so.

Prayer is Work

To pray takes committed concentration, probably more concentration than anything else we do. While we aim to become more relaxed in our inward attentiveness, there will be many times, especially early in the process, and at various times thereafter when we can be left in an arid place.[25] At these times our faith is tested and we are called to concentrate and remain committed until we can be calm again. Commonly the test is to cease reliance on our own efforts and hand the process to God, asking what is the block that needs to be dealt with. The process described by Rex Ambler in *The Light to Live By* can be especially helpful at these times.[26]

We are all prone to peaceful day-dreaming; it can be relaxing and often helpful. While acceptable at other times, it is most unhelpful to lapse into day-dreaming during prayer, even though it might seem a calm and peaceful place. In reality it is focussed on our own comfort, not attentiveness to God. As Fox put it: *"Give not way to the lazy, dreaming mind, for it enters into the temptations".*[27]

The extraordinary social reformer John Bellers (1654-1725) had a prayer life deeply rooted in Quaker silence:

> *The silence of a religious and spiritual worship, is not a drowsy, unthinking state of mind, but a sequestering or withdrawing of it from all visible objects and vain imaginations into a fervent praying to or praising the invisible omnipresent God, in His light and love: His light gives wisdom and knowledge and His love gives power and strength to run the ways of His commandments with delight. But except all excesses of the body and all passions of the mind are avoided, through watchfulness, the soul doth not attain true silence.*[28]

The early Quaker experience was that all thoughts come from the mind, the Self, and are intrusions. The aim is for complete, still silence and absence of thoughts. This prayer of quiet is in the end result a spiritual gift, not something we can manufacture, however we have to make the effort to enter this quiet space where the Spirit can work upon us. Roger Hebden wrote in 1655 of the meditative attention required in returning inward and ignoring thoughts:

> *wait for the increase in God, being content of what is made known of him ... every motion that calls upon you to act or speak, do not lend an ear to it ... return in again ... and be not hasty ... but wait that you may know the mind of God....*[29]

Fox's emphasis on staying away from our own thoughts is well summarised in a letter to Elizabeth, Lady Claypole, one of Cromwell's daughters. Part of his advice is "be still a while," for when almost centred, a major intrusion can be stopped in its tracks by just staying still. Hold the mind absolutely still and allow the light to shine on that intrusion until it loses its hold on in our consciousness. Fox's advice is to scan our internal awareness towards the light, looking across the images of confusion or sin or despair. Fox again uses the phrase 'turn thy mind', that is consciously turn the mind and attention away from those intrusions. We try not to allow ourselves to be caught up in these thoughts and images, for then it is too easy for them to engage us in discussion or in imagining outcomes or to derail us with other emotions:

> *Be still and cool in thy own mind and spirit from thy own thoughts, and then thou wilt feel the principle of God to turn thy mind unto the Lord God, whereby thou wilt receive his strength and power from whence all life comes, to allay all tempests, against blusterings and storms...*
>
> *Therefore be still a while from thy own thoughts, searching, desires and imaginations, and be stayed in the principle of God in thee, to stay thy mind upon God, up to God...*

And now as the principle of God in thee hath been transgressed, come to it, to keep thy mind down low, up to the Lord God; and deny thyself. And from thy own will, that is, the earthly, thou must be kept...

What the light doth make manifest and discover, temptations, confusions, distractions, distempers, do not look at the temptations, confusions, corruptions, but at the light which discovers them, that makes them manifest; and with the same light you will feel over them, to receive power to stand against them... For looking down at sin, and corruption, and distraction, you are swallowed up in it; but looking at the light which discovers them, you will see over them. That will give victory; and you will find grace and strength: and there is the first step of peace. [30]

The early Quaker William Shewen, writing in 1683, is wonderfully reassuring because he acknowledges that thoughts do continually arise, yet we are not to feel despondent or guilty. The key is to let them pass without owning them, without becoming ensnared and carried away by them, and that with practice the Light will begin to help us discern them and know them for what they are:

Now you who are a child of light, understand this one thing for your comfort and encouragement ... that notwithstanding a multitude of thoughts do arise in you, and troops thereof attend you, which are in themselves sinful; yet if you join not with them in your mind, will and understanding, they are not your thoughts, neither shall the evil thereof be imputed to you, if you love the light, and keep your mind joined to the Spirit of God, or the appearance of Christ in you, that discovers all temptations unto you, in the very thought and first appearance of them... [31]

This emphasis not just on outward silence, but also on an inward silence is clear in the Journals written by the early Friends. This inward spiritual space heals the divided Self in a process termed the "Unification of Silence" by Howard Brinton. Here is a description, from Brinton's *Quaker Journals*, by George Whitehead (1636-1722):[32]

> *It was out of these, and such our frequently silent meetings, the Lord was pleased to raise up and bring forth living witnesses, faithful ministers and true prophets. ...Oh! thus keeping silence before the Lord and thus drawing near to him in a true silent frame of Spirit, to hear first what the Lord speaks to us before we speak to others.*

We are to approach this inner work attentively, patiently, and lovingly, while refusing to expect anything. In the end we will realise we cannot achieve anything ourselves, no matter how skilled and admired any of us may be in the outer world! The aim in prayer is not to feel good about ourself, nor to feel bad or guilty, but to feel clearer about ourself and God.

Experience shows we should resist any temptation to "help the process along" or speed it up.[33] Any interference can cause the Divine Presence to disappear. We are to give up *all* control by our Self. The modern world does not accept this total resignation easily, though the early Christians and Quakers were very clear on the need for total surrender of our wills to allow God's full working through us. In the words of John Bellers' prayer:

> *Do thou enable us, O Lord, to prostrate ourselves in deep humility before Thee, with our wills subjected and resigned unto Thy holy will in all things. ... Make us, O Lord, what is right in Thy sight, suitable to the beings which Thou hast made us and the stations which Thou hast placed us in, that our tables nor nothing that we enjoy may become a snare unto us; but that the use and strength of all*

that we receive from Thy bountiful hand may be
returned unto Thee.... [34]

The Self, the Ego, as the Monitor, the Reasoner or Justifier, the Doubter, and the Pretender

Beware the Monitor, the Reasoner, or Justifier, the Doubter, and the Pretender. These thoughts are manifestations of our own Self, our own Ego if you will, trying to maintain control of the process. These thoughts need to be dismissed as soon as they become obvious, pushed aside, or even as Fox once advised "trampled underfoot".[35] All of these are testing our trust in God.

These intruding thoughts can come quickly and catch us unawares. Helena Wong describes her own experience poetically:

> *a door opens*
> *and a stray emotion*
> *stalks into your heart*
> *makes its presence known*
> *- whoa!*
> *before you know it*
> *the furniture has been moved around,*
> *the curtains taken down,*
> *and*
> *you can feel*
> *something*
> *going on, but*
> *what's happening?*
> *how*
> *did this feeling*
> *sneak through*
> *where did it come from?* [36]

The Monitor is like a running commentary or narrative. Typical comments may be: "Are we nearly there?" Or: "What will happen next?" Or: "This is not as good as last time," for which the subtext is: "I want to know what is happening so I can record and report it". The Self wishes to monitor and, if possible, to control the process. Gradually we find we can catch these as they appear, though at first they take over without our realising it—and we simply have to return to a central still position as soon as we become aware of them.

The Reasoner and Justifier will respond immediately to promptings of the Spirit by saying internally such things as: "Yes good idea, but not today because..." Or perhaps: "Yes but, there are other ways of looking at this issue, for instance last year..." Or: "MY own experience says..." Or: "You are too tired or busy now, it is not working, leave it now and it will be better tomorrow". All of these are subtexts for the Self wishing to maintain some control of what happens. After all if we allow the Spirit to fully rule our lives, there is no role left for the Self, and the Self is not going to let this happen lightly.

> [W]atch to feel the savour of life in thy heart day by day, and therein to feel leadings and drawings from the life, suitable to thy state; for in this savour, and in these drawings, rises the true light, which leads into the way of life. And then watch against the reasonings and situations which the enemy will raise in thy mind who will strive to make thee a judge over these drawings; whereas the light, which ariseth in the savour and the drawings, is thy King (though in this low appearance), and not to be judged by the mind, thoughts and reasonings, but to judge them all down, and be bowed unto and obeyed by thee.[37]

The Doubter is just that, the voice that says within us "You will never make it"; "I would not do that because you may find yourself in trouble or get hurt"; or "I am not good or strong enough to do that". A particular voice to me is the implication that the absence of constructive thought is just so BORING—why not focus my attention is something worthwhile thinking about! If we are the sort of person who is good at, even prides oneself in, rational analysis and logical progression through a problem, then this thought that prayer is boring is an effective way to interrupt our meditation. Yet it is just that—just another thought. The rational thinking can be done later; for that intrusion is a temptation to desert the practice of prayer, to abort the attention to God. The subtext for these voices is the mind, the Self, wanting to maintain influence and control, and using our natural fears and hesitancies to advantage. Some of these fears may be of losing status or possessions, and are underlain by a mild avarice or vainglory.

The Pretender has a way of quickly transforming God's wonderful work within us into an assumption it is really our qualities that have enabled this to happen. Early Quaker writings called this role the Boaster. The voice re-frames the instruction of the Spirit into (perhaps) an internal mini-video of ourselves doing the action, and receiving warm approval of our good role in doing so. There can be self-satisfaction, a pride in having done the Spirit's bidding. The Self is making a play to take some or all of the credit for what was in fact God's doing. For even as we undertake God's work, we have to remember it is by God's grace and energy and power in life that we do this, not of our own accord. Yet the Self or Ego loves to pretend it has been influential and achieved this, which in reality is total nonsense.

Our Pretending Self is very inclined to add words and explain what the Spirit has just revealed:

> *Every word of God is pure; ...Add thou not unto his words, lest he reprove thee, and thou be found a liar.* (Proverbs 30: 5-6)

The basis in pride is obvious. These are the examples within us for which the cries of warnings are given:

> *O ye sons of men how long will ye turn my glory into shame.* (Psalm 4: 2)

Who changed the truth of God into a lie, and worshipped and served the creature more than the Creator... (Romans 1: 25)

The Pretender will also raise innumerable little issues to be solved. Resist the temptation to enter into inner debate about these issues, for if we solve one, another will appear. The list is endless. None of these are relevant, not even the ones of apparently deep spiritual significance. They are all symptoms of the Self wanting to understand, to be involved, to set the scene, to influence the outcome. Their principal damage is to undermine trust in God.

There is another insidious behaviour. The Pretender will even pretend to be the voice of the Spirit, whispering consoling answers, pretending to give helpful advice, leading you into a "deep and meaningful conversation," which is in reality nothing more than talking to our Self.

Many writers who describe their own spiritual journey record these tempting diversions and the extended struggle to pass through them, a process of inner stripping and re-patterning. Here is the written evidence from Augustine of Hippo from around 380 AD, and, much later, the experience of the Quaker Stephen Crisp around 1659:

I was about twenty-six or twenty-seven years old. Sweet Truth, although I was straining to catch the sound of your secret melody, I deafened the ears of my heart by allowing my mind to twist and turn among these material possessions of my imagination. As I pondered over beauty and proportion, all the time I wanted to stand still and listen to you ... but this I could not do, because the voice of my own error called me away ... and I was dragged down and down by the weight of my own pride.[38]

About the year 1659, I often felt the aboundings of the love of God in my heart, and a cry to stand up to his will.... This love and tenderness and bowels of compassion wrought so in me that it extended even to all men on the whole face of the earth. ...[Crisp was being called to undertake a journey in the ministry] *But when that came to pass I found all enemies were not slain indeed; for the strivings, strugglings, reasonings and disputings against the command of God that I then met withal cannot be told or numbered! Oh! how I would have pleaded my own inability, the care of my family, my service in that particular meeting, and many more things, and all that I might have been excused from this one thing which was come upon me, that I thought not of, or looked not for.*[39]

Early Friends knew all these diversions well. They experienced the many subtle ways the Self can undermine our growing allegiance to the divine voice within us. That is why they advised to stay away from ALL thoughts.

They understood that the Self has two main strategies to divert us from prayer. The first is to engender a roving mind, seeking all sorts of thoughts and mental opportunities. Some have called this 'outrunning your Guide'. The second, if the first fails, is doubt, perhaps despair, and the urge to revert to our more comfortable worldly knowledge and existence. Both these trains of thought are diversions. The real path to God and peace, the narrow path, lies between them, neither to one side nor to the other, and is to be followed with careful and diligent effort. Here is James Nayler, in 1660:

Wherefore run not with that which is in haste, but lie down in that which is meek, lowly and patient. ... For a nature there is which runs out for help, and raveneth abroad to be satisfied, which God will famish; and this will lead to the mind, if it be followed, and will hunt about and murmur if it not be satisfied...

But in this work take heed you not be betrayed with that spirit, for it is very subtle, to run to the one hand or the other, either into the eagerness and haste, which is its first way after convincement; or else, when it gets not its ends there, then into sloth and idle carelessness... but a straight way there is betwixt these ... which is diligent, watchful, patient meekness, feeling the godly principle moving and following it in faith and obedience in all things ... for only the diligent mind holdeth the true living treasure, but the slothful and disobedient are leaking vessels.[40]

The Devil?

The opposing voice within which seeks to divert our inward attention from being still has been variously identified by human beings as the Devil, Satan, Lucifer, the Adversary, the Enemy, Snake, the Tempter, the Evil One, the Wolf of Hate, and many other imaginary and mythical creatures. These images are caricatures, allegorical stories that are then commonly backed up with extraordinary images and legendary tales. However there is a profound error in such thinking because it allows people to blame this as a foreign influence within them. The spiritual journey then becomes a struggle between myself and this "evil" power. The main work of the spiritual journey can become overly focussed on this foreign power rather than on the divine presence.

The reader may dislike this Devil/Satan/Lucifer terminology. If so, ignore it, but what we cannot ignore is the terrifying destructiveness which can infect and possess the human spirit. It can enter politely, plausibly, respectably, even religiously, germinate quietly and peacefully for a while, then erupt in savagery and destruction.[41]

Some early Quakers used these inherited images, but the most profound writings echo Buddhist philosophy, in which the opposing voices are the cravings and attachments desired by the Self or Ego. This Self, a self-centeredness, places a veil over that of God within us, in Fox's words "which would cloud and veil from the presence of Christ".[42]

The Quaker way then is to focus not on the dark and terrible images, because this gives those images more power, but to focus on the Light within. Hence Buddhist advice, on becoming aware of any thoughts, is to return to the breathing without any engagement with the intruding thoughts. Hence George Fox's clear advice to stay away from all thoughts, and his primary teaching to "stand still in the Light".

A very natural part of our human condition is self-interest in our basic survival and well-being. Yet the natural self-centredness can also be extended into very unhelpful inner thoughts of self-congratulation, self-justification and self-pity. It takes some time and some divine assistance to handle these tendencies within us. All need to be abandoned as quickly as possible with no regrets.

Self-congratulation was recognised by ancient mystics as the sin of vainglory. It involves inwardly recounting stories and examples of where we have done well, whereas any spiritual progress is the result of divine enabling. In the modern age, the emphasis on promoting self-esteem is a spiritual trap. It may be a useful, even essential, step for damaged individuals to take on the way to recovery. However Quaker prayer has emphasised a reliance upon God, not a reliance on our own power and self-confidence.

Self-justification is characterised by judgements or criticism of others, and some inward reflection will generally show quickly that in such behaviours we have to admit we too have been similarly at fault. It is so easy to project our hidden or unacceptable difficulties and errors onto others. These judgements are so often a mirror of ourselves. In making judgements and criticisms we have simply protected our own Ego by laying the fault at another's door. In some circumstances this judgemental attitude assumes a heightened degree of enlightened self-righteousness. Images flood our mind of why we are right and that person is wrong and why God requires us to point out their sins and mete out correction. Paul noted that false prophets can appear as "angels of light".[43] One name for the traditional Devil is 'Lucifer' meaning the bearer of light, because these bright inner images of self-justification can be strongly associated with judgement and even the impulse to punish others.

Self-pity places us as the victim, even of the most trivial situations, such as a misunderstood casual remark. A sense of being personally affronted or aggrieved, especially unjustifiably aggrieved, is a common manifestation. There are times we have been badly treated, and there is a need to set the record straight and even seek reparation. However it is also very easy to make use of these occasions in our own self-interest and to inwardly inflame a sense of child-like hurt with the seeking of a justifiable punishment for the other party. Self-pity is really the obverse of the coin of self-congratulation; it is the same Ego requiring attention. In one, the Ego is over inflated and basking in its own false glory; in the other the Ego feels wounded and is manipulating for more attention.

Self-pity may also appear as a complaining attitude to life, close to blaming God for the worldly or spiritual situation in which we find ourselves. Yet later on we may come to recognise that each of these times were important learning and growing experiences. This is not to say that God deliberately sets such trials for us; but that God does recognise life always presents difficult situations and it is up to us, no matter what our station in life, to seek divine guidance moment-by-moment on how to handle them. The complaining attitude from our Self obliterates a sense of trust and gratefulness.

Any Self-centred commentary can be very subtle. It is often worth stopping inwardly to ask if there is any hint of desire for worldly recognition, which reveals that a thought is not a prompting from the house of the Lord, but emanates from the false temple of the Self.

The life of prayer gradually dispenses with these manifestations of the Self, and assumes a continuing dependence, trust and acknowledgement of God. It can be a long journey to complete faith in God and divine providence.

What Does Self-denial Mean in Practice?

In prayer, at first, self-denial means refusing to give in to the wishes of the Self or Ego, those attempts of the Self to be involved in commenting on and advising on the process and progress of our spiritual life. That the Self might have a dual role with God in determining and feeding our inward prayer life is an absurd, impertinent and laughable proposition. The only thing the Self does is get in the way. The Self is a veil before God.

> *Early Friends had a vision, made tangible through their own personal experiences of inwardly crucifying their own self-centredness in order to submit to the Life of Christ resurrected within them.*[44]

So self-denial is, firstly, a simple attitude of denying the Self any role in the process of prayer. This may seem strange at first, but must be borne and practised. It is not a huge demand by God, just a different direction from our previous way. God asks for our love and attention.

Then self-denial moves to the position of ceasing to ask for joy and consolation, ceasing to expect less difficulty and more fruit, for less dryness and more sweetness. These needs are illusions inserted by the Self. God is not to be found in the satisfying of the Self's needs. God is to be found in the abandoning of these needs, and in a desire to love and please God. In fact the Divine Presence is with every one of us every moment, whether we are aware of it or not.

Self-denial becomes an ability to cease asking for an intellectual understanding. It is a mistake to think we can understand and then do it. The reverse is true — we do it and then God grants understanding. Self-denial requires us to follow the promptings and leadings of the Spirit in all our thoughts and works, even when we have previously done it another way. It is a pretence to think "I know better". We have to be open to changing our previous habits.

While many have learnt in previous church experiences that self-denial means a continuing disregard for one's own wellbeing, this is wrong. Self-denial is not continuing enslavement to the demands of others; Self-denial is a loving obedience to God.

Yet the Self does not let go easily, and it is only through the divine working within us that we are finally able to discern clearly the voice of Truth from that of the Stranger who seeks to divert us. We gradually find it easier and then become changed in a way which we did not do ourselves, but which nevertheless happens within us. Gradually and mysteriously we are given an ability to discern and to stay obedient to God's calling, which we did not previously have.

George Fox wrote an early Epistle in 1652 to Friends about this Quaker method of standing still in the Light, of standing still mentally and not allowing the mind to pursue or debate thoughts, as a way to release the hold of the Self and enter more deeply into the divine presence.[45]

Epistle X. (10)
To Friends, to stand still in trouble, and see the strength of the Lord.

Friends, — Whatever ye are addicted to, the tempter

*will come in that thing; and when he can trouble
you, then he gets advantage over you, and then ye
are gone. Stand still in that which is pure, after ye
see yourselves; and then mercy comes in. After thou
seest thy thoughts, and the temptations, do not think,
but submit; and then power comes. Stand still in that
which shows and discovers; and there doth strength
immediately come. And stand still in the light, and
submit to it, and the other will be hushed and gone;
and then content comes. And when temptations and
troubles appear, sink down in that which is pure,
and all will be hushed, and fly away. Your strength
is to stand still, after ye see yourselves; whatsoever
ye see yourselves addicted to, temptations,
corruption, uncleanness, &c. then ye think ye shall
never overcome. And earthly reason will tell you,
what ye shall lose; hearken not to that, but stand
still in the light that shows them to you, and then
strength comes from the Lord, and help contrary to
your expectation. Then ye grow up in peace, and no
trouble shall move you. David fretted himself, when
he looked out; but when he was still, no trouble
could move him. When your thoughts are out,
abroad, then troubles move you. But come to stay
your minds upon that spirit which was before the
letter; here ye learn to read the scriptures aright. If
ye do any thing in your own wills, then ye tempt
God; but stand still in that power which brings
peace. G. F.*

Our job in prayer is to be totally open and trusting to what
God asks of us and to where God directs us. This committed,
inward trust, a lack of personal expectation, opens up a
wonderland of inner experience and guidance. When we
submit inwardly we can be confident that no matter what issue
is placed before us outwardly, God's presence will be with us
and provide the answers, the directions for the way forward.
Prayer is a wonderful investment in the future.

The scriptural advices, well known to early Friends, for this approach are based on Jesus' promise of the coming of the Holy Spirit:

> *And I will pray the Father, and he shall give you another Comforter, that he may abide with you for ever; Even the Spirit of truth; whom the world cannot receive, because it seeth him not, neither knoweth him: but ye know him; for he dwelleth with you, and shall be in you.* (John 14:16-17)

> *But the Comforter, which is the Holy Ghost, whom the Father will send in my name, he shall teach you all things, and bring all things to your remembrance, whatsoever I have said unto you.* (John 14:26)

This Inward Guide will bring us into greater understanding of God, a journey that requires us to act in truth (1 John 3: 19-21):

> *And hereby we know that we are of the truth, and shall assure our hearts before him. For if our heart condemn us, God is greater than our heart, and knoweth all things. Beloved, if our heart condemn us not, then we have confidence towards God.*

Having said beware of these intrusive thoughts, it is very important to test leadings and promptings and not just rush off into public action at the first impulse. For these impulses, we have well-established tests developed by Quakers and other traditional Christians.

Rest assured, the inner guide will *never* move us in prayer to start thinking. Later we may find our thinking processes are clearer and we are more easily clear about decisions; however any weighing of the pros and cons is not the work to do in prayer. Consider the advice given once to Rufus Jones:

> *Trembling he rose to speak, and then began with a
> phrase now so familiar in Friends meetings, 'Since
> sitting in this meeting I have been thinking...' At the
> rise of meeting an elderly Friend in the plain dress
> ... took him aside and said, 'I was grieved at what
> thou said in meeting. Thou said that since sitting in
> the meeting thou hadst been thinking. Thou
> shouldest not have been thinking.'[46]*

We will not know what is to happen next or where we will be
led in prayer. An attitude of "Dear God, show me what you
will" is the way.[47] This submission, this surrendering of the
Self to the Light is practised in prayer so that it becomes a
basis of the life lived.[48]

> *So I tarried here a great while, till my wife cried, 'We'se
> all be ruined: what is thee ganging stark mad to follow
> t'silly Quakers?' Here I struggled and cried, and begged
> of my Guide to stay and take my pace: and presently my
> wife was convinced. 'Well,' says she, 'now follow thy
> Guide, let come what will. The Lord hath done abundance
> for us: we will trust in Him.'*

Step Two: Yield Mentally, and Accept that True Prayer and Ministry are the Work of God not the Human Mind.

We are well aware that vocal ministry in meeting for worship
is supposed to come at the prompting of the Spirit. Yet we
may think that surely just a few thoughts of mine are all right,
after all I am sure I know what is important and what that
person needs; I know what is best for this situation, so I will
sit quietly and ask God to make sure it happens.
Unfortunately, for us (!), that is not what early Quakers did.
These first Friends were acutely aware that the power within
them was divine, not human.[49]

Fox's primary message in prayer was to stay away from all
thoughts, and especially to leave off from all rehearsed and
practised prayers and liturgies, to be silent, and have our

inward attention "stand still in the Light," and then to follow the Light. John Lampen gives a very good summary. [50]

Fox's advice is that prayer is a matter of waiting:

> *Therefore, all wait patiently upon the Lord, whatsoever condition you be in; wait in the grace and truth that comes by Jesus; for if ye so do, there is a promise to you, and the Lord God will fulfil it in you.* [51]

> *None that is upon the earth shall ever come to God, but as they come to that of God in them—the Light that God has enlightened them with. That is it which must guide every one's mind up to God ... The Spirit leads to wait upon God in silence, and to receive from God.* [52]

A similar message and instruction was given by William Smith in 1663:

> *It has been a Common Observation through Ages and Generations, to perform something as a duty unto God by way of Prayer ... it is manifest that the way of Prayer, as it is now commonly used, observed and practised in the Common Worship, is not true Prayer, but a bare formality, and not only so, but also contradictory, and so is not performed with right understanding. ...So all must come to the Spirit of God, by the Spirit to be ordered, and cease from their own words and from their own time, and learn to be silent until the Spirit give them utterance; for the Lord is weary of all Formality and Hypocrisie, and ... hath no pleasure in such performances...* [53]

William Penn emphasises the role of the Spirit in preparing the heart for such worship, [54] and that is why we must refrain from our own wordy inputs:

*True worship can only come from a heart prepared
by the Lord. ...And whatever prayer be made, or
doctrine be uttered, and not from the preparation of
the Holy Spirit, it is not acceptable with God; nor
can it be the true evangelical worship, which is in
spirit and truth; that is by the preparation and aid of
the Holy Spirit. For what is a heap of pathetical
words to God Almighty; or the dedication of any
place or time to him?...*

*But it may be asked, how shall this preparation be
obtained?*

*I answer; by waiting patiently, yet watchfully and
intently, upon God. ...Thou must not think thy own
thoughts nor speak thy own words, which indeed is
the silence of the holy cross, but be sequestered from
all the confused imaginations that are apt to throng
and press upon the mind in those holy retirements.
Think not to overcome the Almighty by the most
composed matter cast into the aptest phrase. No,
one groan, one sigh, from a wounded soul, an heart
touched with true remorse, a sincere and godly
sorrow, which is the work of God's spirit, excels and
prevails with God. Wherefore, stand still in thy
mind, wit to feel something divine, to prepare and
dispose thee to worship God truly and acceptably.
Thus taking up the cross, and shutting the doors and
windows of the soul against everything that would
interrupt this attendance upon God, how pleasant
soever the object be in itself, or however lawful or
needful at another season, the power of the Almighty
will break in, his Spirit will prepare the heart, that it
may offer up an acceptable sacrifice. It is he that
discovers to the soul its wants, and presses them
upon it; and when it cries, he alone can supply them.
Petitions, not springing from such a sense and
preparation, are formal and fictitious; they are not*

true: for men pray in their own blind desires and not
in the will of God; and his ear is stopped to them. [55]

The required watchfulness was attested by many early
Quakers – Robert Barclay, Elizabeth Bathurst, Stephen Crisp,
Margaret Fell, George Fox, Sarah Jones, James Naylor,
William Penn, Isaac Penington, William Smith. Here is Penn
in 1669:

Thus it was, that where once nothing was examined,
nothing went unexamined. Every thought must come
to judgment, and the rise and tendency of it be well
approved, before they allowed it any room in their
minds. There was no fear of entertaining enemies for
friends, whilst this strict guard was kept upon the
very wicket of the soul. [56]

John Bellers, the Quaker political and social activist on behalf
of the poor, wrote a pamphlet in 1703 *Watch unto Prayer*.
Braithwaite introduces Bellers with these words:

Bellers tells us that watching is as needful to the
soul as breathing is to the body: it is the mark of life,
and its absence means the dominion of the sensual
and the earthly, which tends to death. It is the
preparation for bringing every thought into captivity
to the obedience of Christ, "and he that thinks no
evil will be sure to act none".

He that keeps not a watch upon the thoughts of his
heart is much out of the way; for, though he could
imitate the best of forms, he is but of the outward
court; it being impossible to worship God in the
beauty of holiness with an irregular mind.

Watchfulness out of meetings is the best preparation
for worship within; neither hearing the best
preachers, nor a bare turning the thoughts inward

when one comes into a meeting, is the true spiritual
worship, for the heart within may be a den of
darkness, but he that watches in the light will be led
into the new Jerusalem, where God and the Lamb
are both the light and the temple to worship in, and
nothing that defiles can enter.[57]

The first two stanzas of The Dhamma from the Buddhist faith
contain the same warning and advice:

Mind is the cause of all that we are; mind is the
basis and they are all shaped by the mind. If one
speaks or acts with an impure mind, then suffering
follows one as the wagon wheel the hoof of the ox.

Mind is the cause of all that we are; mind is the
basis and they are all shaped by the mind. If one
speaks or acts with a pure mind, then happiness
follows one like one's ever present shadow.

The abundant testimony of early Quakers was that "the Lord
did show me the way" and that "the Lord did break down my
resistance".[58] In other words we cannot ourselves do this work
of purifying our hearts and approaching God. The power to do
this is not our own. This work is done partly by God alone,
and partly by God strengthening each of us within. It requires
repentance and humility.[59] Early Quaker letters and journals
are replete with admissions of the inner stripping required by
each individual.

For example, here are the words firstly of Stephen Crisp,
secondly of Isaac Penington, and thirdly of the modern
Quaker Sandra Cronk:

So after long travel, strong cries, and many bitter
tears and groans, I found a little hope springing in
me, that the Lord in his own time would bring forth
his Seed, even his elect Seed, the seed of his
covenant, to rule in me; and this was given me at a

*time when a sense of my own unworthiness had so
overwhelmed me in sorrow and anguish ... and I
was taught to wait on God, and to eat and drink in
fear and watchfulness,...*[60]

*And O, know that your strength lies not in
yourselves, not in any thing ye can do of yourselves:
but in God's living principle of truth, wherein he
appears and whereby he works in your hearts.
Therefore wait for the Lord's visiting and appearing
to you there, and making your souls acquainted with
him therein.*[61]

*By facing the darkness, we confront that empty place
inside each of us. ...Our strivings after meaning and
purpose—indeed—after God—have brought us to
the end of ourselves and ... we face nothing or so it
seems. In that empty place we can at last know that
which transcends ourselves. ...We come to God
alone. ...We begin to recognise a deeper conversion
or turning to God which takes place in the dark
night. A profound re-patterning begins in us. The re-
patterning can happen because the old structure of
our lives has been broken up. All those good but
creaturely pillars will no longer serve as the centre
of our lives. Now that they are taken away, a new
centre can emerge. That new centre is God. This
new centre is not simply an intellectually or
emotionally based faith in God. The dark night
journey has re-shaped our activity patterns, our
value system, and our whole being so that God is the
functional centre of our living.*[62]

Rex Ambler also describes this process as one of the steps of
his Light Group meditation for the individual:

*When the answer comes welcome it. It may be
painful, or difficult to believe with your normal
conscious mind, but if it is the truth you will*

*recognise it immediately and realise that it is
something you need to know. Trust the light, Say yes
to it. Submit to it. It will then begin to heal you. It
will show you new possibilities for your life. It will
show you the way through. So however bad the news
may seem at first, accept it and let its truth pervade
your whole being.*[63]

Fox wrote vividly of his own experience, when the Light
began to appear in him, of how he was examined so
thoroughly that all those parts which were acceptable before
God were made clear, and all those parts which were not
acceptable became manifest, and had to be allowed to die—
his analogy was being inwardly crucified.[64]

The early apostles and later Christian saints wrote of the same
need to retire inwardly and thoroughly examine ourselves,
allowing the Spirit free rein to expose and assess our
innermost workings, to show us which are acceptable and
which unacceptable in the eyes of God. This inward re-
assessment can be quite a severe process, and the writings
above show early Quakers had this experience. Further, all
emphasise this is not a process of mental or rational thinking,
for it is only the Spirit who can know how God sees us. Here
are two passages: one from St Paul, and one from the
Franciscan monk St Bonaventure (1221-1274).

*We do, however, speak a message of wisdom among
the mature, but not the wisdom of this age or of the
rulers of this age, who are coming to nothing. No,
we speak of God's secret wisdom, a wisdom that has
been hidden and that God destined for our glory
before time began. None of the rulers of this age
understood it, for if they had, they would not have
crucified the Lord of glory. However, as it is
written: 'No eye has seen, no ear has heard, no
mind has conceived what God has prepared for
those who love him, '*[65] *but God has revealed it to us
by his Spirit. The Spirit searches all things, even the*

deep things of God. For who among men knows the thoughts of a man except the man's spirit within him? In the same way no one knows the thoughts of God except the Spirit of God.[66]

First of all, ...[one] who wishes to rise to the summit of the perfect life should start at the level of her own self. Forgetting the material world, she must enter the hidden recesses of her conscience, there to explore, examine, and weigh with attentive care all her faults, habits, affections, and deeds, all her sins, both past and present. ...Oh how dangerous it is for a religious to be inquisitive about many things while ignoring her own self! ...Therefore, totally immersed in the senses, it [the human mind] is unable to re-enter into itself as into the likeness of God.[67]

Barclay, in his *Apology*, is very clear that our spiritual rescue is in the hands of God, though our "condemnation" is entirely in our own hands. This is not any easy concept for most of us!

That as the grace and light in all is sufficient to save all, and of its own nature would save all; so it strives and wrestles with all in order to save them; he that resists its striving, is the cause of his own condemnation; he that resists it not, it becomes his salvation: for that in him that is saved, the working is of the grace and not of the man; and it is a passiveness rather than an act; though afterwards, as a man is wrought upon, there is a will raised in him, by which he becomes a co-worker with grace [68] *...*

These instructions from early Quakers remind me of the implications in other writings on prayer, such as *The Cloud of Unknowing* (Ch. 2), namely that we are to respond to God's promptings within us: *"How sluggish and slothful the soul that does not respond to Love's attraction and invitation"*. The required inwardness and holy obedience are also keenly expressed in the psalms, such as David's realisation that he could not expiate sin by going to the temple and following some established ritual:

> *For thou desirest not sacrifice; else I would give it:*
> *thou desirest not in burnt offering. The sacrifices of*
> *God are a broken spirit: a broken and contrite heart,*
> *O God, thou wilt not despise.* (Psalm 51: 16-17)[69]

The established church services have emphasised an attitude that prayer is based on our own words, both in formal liturgies and also our own petitions. We have been bred up in a "customary and formal way," as William Smith noted.[70] The early Quakers asserted these spoken words were both ineffective and unacceptable to God. Quaker prayer is based on stilling all our own words and becoming attentive to the holy voice and Light within. We are to stop our inner speaking and cultivate an attitude of inward listening. We are to wait patiently for God to communicate with us, for there is nothing we can do to manufacture this response from God.

Fox writes repeatedly in his *Journal* that his teaching was to "Keep within," "turn to the Christ who had enlightened them," or "turn to the Light".[71] In these words he was saying that we should direct our attention inwards, away from our normal thoughts and behaviours, and seek inspiration and leadings from within. This is not an immediately easy thing to do, and requires some practice.

Step Three: Accept and Love the Light, Following Jesus' Teachings

The great strength and power and life of early Friends derived from their total commitment to Jesus as the source of the Light in their consciences.[72] We might like to think otherwise today because such total commitment clashes with our modern ways of self-control and rational thinking, for it impinges on our own freedom to make up our own minds. It is as if we expect to be an internal democracy where a range of voices and options can each have their say, and then we get to decide which is best. The Kingdom of God is not a democracy.

Many modern people have rejected the established churches and doctrines. The early Quakers did it 350 years ago, only with more vigour and with greater persecution than in the comfort we enjoy today. The key point is the early Quakers rejected the Church—they did NOT reject the teachings and spiritual guidance of Jesus. They knew that Jesus' ministry had been misrepresented and distorted by the Church. Fox considered most priests as being in apostasy.[73]

The first Friends felt they had re-discovered the way of the Apostles. A description of early Christian worship sounds very like a Quaker meeting with its emphasis on silent waiting, the opportunity for individual ministry (prophesy), careful weighing, and the lack of creeds and liturgy (1 Corinthians 14: 26-33 NIV):

> *What then shall we say, brothers and sisters? When you come together, each of you has a hymn, or a word of instruction, a revelation, a tongue or an interpretation. Everything must be done so that the church may be built up. If anyone speaks in a tongue, two—or at the most three—should speak, one at a time, and someone must interpret. If there is no interpreter, the speaker should keep quiet in the church and speak to himself and to God.*

> *Two or three prophets should speak, and the others should weigh carefully what is said. And if a revelation comes to someone who is sitting down, the first speaker should stop. For you can all prophesy in turn so that everyone may be instructed and encouraged. The spirits of prophets are subject to the control of prophets. For God is not a God of disorder but of peace—as in all the congregations of the Lord's people.*

Francis Howgill wrote in 1672 of the early Quaker experience
in his essay on the life of Edward Burrough, emphasising the
patient surrender of themselves to the Light, without any
words spoken, and of the glorious visitations they received.
The immediacy of the divine presence among them was
astounding:

> *Testimony reached unto all our Consciences, and
> entered into the in-most part of our Hearts, which
> drove us to a narrow search, and to a diligent
> inquisition concerning our state, which we came to
> see through the Light of Christ Jesus, which was
> testified of, and found it to be even what it was
> testified of; and the Lord of Heaven and Earth we
> found to be near at hand; and as we waited upon
> him in pure Silence, our Minds out of all things, his
> Dreadful Power, and Glorious Majesty, and
> Heavenly Presence appeared in our Assemblies,
> when there was no Language, Tongue nor Speech
> from any Creature, and the Kingdom of Heaven did
> gather us, and catch us all, as in a Net; and his
> Heavenly Power at one time drew many Hundreds to
> Land, that we came to know a place to stand in, and
> what to wait in; and the Lord appeared daily to us,
> to our Astonishment, Amazement, and great
> Admiration, insomuch that we often said one unto
> another, with great joy of Heart, What, is the
> Kingdom of God come to be with men?*[74]

The Quaker instructions were to "Turn to the Light," to "Mind
the Light," and to "Love the Light," that is to pay great
attention to this inward Light that illumines our conscience.
Even if in prayer we are filled with darkness, we are aware of
that darkness, almost as if the darkness is like the night before
dawn, when we are dimly aware that it is still night. There is a
faint illumination within each of us. However our conscience
is where this Light first shows, as checks on our behaviour.
We can over-ride these checks or follow them.

At first our measure[75] of the Light is small, and the Quaker experience was that spiritual progress came by surrendering to what the Light asks of us. This process takes deep commitment, without opting out of the process. In the first of the following two quotes Sarah Jones (1650) emphasises the attentiveness required to keep our focus on the measure of life we have, so that the unseen divine work can assist us. In the second, William Dewsbury (1655) notes that if we obey the Light, the life will increase.

> [S]ink down into that measure of life that ye have received, and go not out with your in-looking at what is contrary to you, for if you do you will miss of the power that should destroy it, for as ye keep in that which is pure, which is the eternal word of the Lord, which is nigh in your hearts, it will work and operate so, that it will overcome what is contrary.[76]

> Return within everyone in particular; examine your hearts, and mind the Light in your conscience, and it will always let you see where your hearts are, and what they delight in, for it is the heart the Lord requires; ... there is your teacher within you, the light of your consciences; loving it, and obeying it, is your life; hating it and disobeying it, is your condemnation:[77]

William Shewen in 1683 summarised the process as follows, describing the dual work involved as the initial task set for each of us, and in turn our efforts are enabled by the work of the Light:

> Now at the first step towards restoration and everlasting happiness, you are required to turn your mind from the darkness in which you dwell, to the light, eye or Spirit of God, and to decline the power of Satan that works in the darkness, and embrace the Power of God; and when you doest but begin to do so, you wilt find the scales to fall from your eyes by

degrees, and the veil to be taken off your heart, and
the fetters and chains of darkness to be loosed, and
the prison doors opened; so when your candle is
lighted, and your eye opened, you wilt discern your
way out, and see the angel of the lord go before you,
and guide you in the same; ...and as you love this
light, you wilt be enabled by it to divide thought and
thought, and begin to make conscience of a thought;
and to hate every vain thought, and when you cannot
be easily rid of them, nor remove them from their
old lodging-place, you wilt breathe and cry to the
Lord, as one of old did .... Now the only way to
dislodge them, and to be rid of their company, is to
show them no countenance, make no provision for
them, give them no entertainment, but by the light of
God, which discovers them to be your enemies,
judge them, and keep your mind exercised in the
light and Power of God, that it is turned to; and in
your thoughts and imaginations, give them no
regard; and though they do and may arise, pursue
and compass you about like bees, yet you, keeping
your eye fixed in the light and Power of God, which
is as near to you as your thoughts are, and shows
them unto you, you wilt see them, in due time
scattered as chaff before a fierce wind, and
destroyed as stubble before a devouring fire.[78]

George Fox's ministry and that of other early Quakers was
delivered with evangelic fervour to thousands of people
throughout Britain, and centred on a teaching for seekers to
"turn (inward) to the Light of Christ in their hearts," for Jesus
"was come now to teach his people again himself by his
power and spirit".[79]

This Light and Spirit of Christ are already at work within us
drawing us toward God. We are to turn our attention inward
and to be willing to learn from, and respond to what is
revealed in our hearts. The Light most commonly starts as a

faint, inner awareness. Yet we will be struck by a deep honesty, the Truth of the awareness that comes to us.

It is as natural as it is unproductive to wonder if we are doing well or not, for that is focussing on the Self, and we are allowing the thoughts from the Monitor to intrude again. The accent must be on following the Light, seeking God, loving to do what we are led to do, not trying to gauge how far along the journey we are. Our job at first is simply to sit quietly in this inward darkness with its minimal illumination, for that is where God is asking us to be, for reasons not understood by us at the time.

The Light as both Revealer and Healer

The original Quaker experience fitted the early Friends' readings of the scripture, especially the Gospel of John, namely that Jesus is the source of the Inward Light, which shows us two things: what is wrong within us and blocking our way to God, and also what we are to do to be God's instrument in the world. Fox identified within himself "that which would cloud and veil from the presence of Christ".[80] So the value of this Light and what it reveals are paramount. Jesus' teaching set a standard for behaviour and decisions so that careful reading of the gospel stories, the parables and miracles has as much to offer as food for our spiritual growth.

The Quaker experiences and understanding were that this inward presence of God is always present and is to be followed diligently to the exclusion of all else. This is an ancient wisdom, the following of divine leading and teaching, while being ready to sideline our own desires:

> *Trust the Lord with all thine heart and lean not unto thine own understanding. In all thy ways acknowledge him, and he shall direct thy paths. Be not wise in thine own eyes: Fear the Lord and depart from evil.* (Proverbs 3:5-7)

This process leads to an inner cleansing and purification, " *My son, despise not the chastening of the Lord: neither be weary of his correction* ". (Proverbs 3:11)

Here are three early Quaker writings that make the same point about the inward presence of God in their own words: one from Fox (1654) referring to Jesus, the second from James Parnell (1675), and the third referring to the Light of Christ by Elizabeth Bathurst (1679):

> *I am the light of the world, and enlightens every one that commeth into the world: Christ hath enlightened every one that comes into the world; thou that loves that light which Christ hath enlightened thee withal, thou brings thy workes to the light, that thy deeds may be proved that they were wrought in God; and he that walks in the light, there is no occasion of stumbling in him, it teacheth righteousness and holiness, ...thou that loves it, here's thy teacher, when thou art walking abroad, it's present with thee in thy bosome thou need not say Loe here, or loe there, and as thou liest in bed it is present to teach thee, and judge thy wandering mind which would wander abroad, and thy thoughts and imaginations ... for the first step of peace is to stand still in the light, which discovers things contrary to it, for power and strength to stand against that nature which the light discovers; here grace grows...*[81]

> *And thou who art willing to follow this, and to be guided by this, shalt need no man to teach thee, but it will be a teacher unto thee, teaching and directing thee in righteousness, purity and holiness; and if thou art diligent, keeping thy mind within, with an ear open to the pure voice, thou shalt find it with thee wheresoever thou art, in the fields, in thy bed, in markets, in company, or wheresoever thou art; ... it will be present with thee, and will check thee and*

*condemn thee for that which no outward eye can
see, and will cleanse thy heart from lust, and deceit,
and uncleanness and will purify thy heart, and make
it a fit temple for purity to dwell in; and then thy
sacrifices will be pure, which come from a pure
heart, and the Lord will accept them.*[82]

*...that one Eternal; Principle, to wit, the Light of
Christ manifest in the Conscience, ...leads into a
Heavenly Order, ...according to the diversity of its
Gifts, whereby Man comes not to be at liberty in his
own Will, but bound again to God, which is the true
significance of the word Religion:*[83]

Fox's first step is "Stand still in the light"—sometimes this
leads to a wonderful "opening" or understanding, sometimes
to a divine reproving. Do not recoil from what it shows you,
or deny the import.[84] Wait and discover what it is showing
you, both about your inner errors and your wrongdoings, and
also what to do:

*Therefore, all wait patiently upon the Lord,
whatsoever condition you be in; wait in the grace
and truth that comes by Jesus; for if ye do, there is a
promise to you, and the Lord God will fulfil it in
you.*[85]

It is very easy to resist this process and to find "good" reasons
to do so. However that is a futile path. It takes some practice
and commitment to stay with the light and see what happens.
The key is a genuine inward humility. The experience of those
who have done this in trust is that you need not be afraid of
what will happen. God is loving, and reveals and straightens
us gently, step by step.

Fox mentions this standing still in the Light as the "first step
of peace," while I have put it as the third. My own
interpretation and experience is that we need to practise the
first two steps, of a commitment to centring down and of

yielding, before we get to recognise and experience the Light. By 'first step' my feeling is Fox understood full well that this step begins a process of continuing revelation, and we each must take the first step to start this journey. As William Penn described the Light:

> *That first showed thee thy sins and reproved them,*
> *and enabled thee to deny and resist them ... So that*
> *the cross mystical is that divine grace and power*
> *which crosseth the carnal wills often, and so may be*
> *justly termed the instrument of man's holy dying to*
> *the world and being made conformable to the will of*
> *God. ...The great work and business of the cross in*
> *man is self-denial, a word little understood by the*
> *world, but less embraced by it; yet it must be borne*
> *for all that.*[86]

Margaret Fell made it clear in 1656 that Quaker prayer will result in major changes within you, a process of gradual, relentless, inner transformation for the better:

> *Now Friends, deal plainly with your selves, and let*
> *the eternal Light search you, and try you, for the*
> *good of your souls; for this will deal plainly with*
> *you; it will rip you up, and lay you open, and make*
> *all manifest which lodgeth in you ... by this be*
> *searched and judged, and led and guided;*[87]

The changes required by God were both external and internal. For example there were external changes in habit and behaviour, bringing the outward life into a consistent pattern for early Friends, such as plain dress without the excessive frills of expensive clothes, plain speaking to signify all are equal before God, complete truth in words and dealings with others, and the refusal to engage in violence.

The same necessary inner transformation that leads to an external transformation was foretold by Fox himself in part of a letter written from Launceston prison in Cornwall in 1656:

Bring all into the worship of God. Plough up the fallow ground ... and none are ploughed up but he who comes to the principle of God in him which he hath transgressed. Then he does service to God; then the planting and watering and the increase from God cometh. So the ministers of the Spirit must minister to the Spirit that is transgressed and in prison, which hath been in captivity in everyone; whereby with the same Spirit people must be led out of captivity up to God, ...And this is the word of the Lord God to you all, and a charge to you all in the presence of the living God: be patterns, be examples in all countries, places, islands, nations, wherever you come, that your carriage and life may preach among all sorts of people, and to them; then you will come to walk cheerfully over the world, answering that of God in everyone[88]

However these were not all that was required. Thoughts were also to be cleansed, as testified by Thomas Ellwood in the story of his own life written in 1714:

Now was my former life ripped up, and my sins by degrees were set in order before me. ...Now also did I receive a new law, (an inward law superadded to the outward), the law of the spirit, which wrought in me against all evil, not only in deed, and in word, but even in thought also. ...So that here began to be a way cast up before me for me to walk in, a direct and plain way, so plain that a wayfaring man how weak and simple ... could not err while he continued to walk in it.[89]

The Mental Attitude in Quaker Prayer and its Role in Spiritual Growth

The Quaker method will seem strange to those who have been previously trained in an established church. There are NO formalised prayers. There is no pattern of recitations, no place for well-meaning phrases. The Quaker method is based on total commitment to waiting in silence; and we start in a dark, inward silence.

The commitment to silent waiting on the Spirit is the prime Quaker testimony. The early Quakers made a major break with the established forms of worship and social custom; not that they were the only alternative seekers at the time, but because they persisted and brought this form of prayer to fruition, changing much in the society around them. It is a radical step, even for us today, to commit to "no more words and thinking, just wait in silence". All the other works and testimonies of those first Friends flowed from this single commitment.

In practice, many find it helpful to have a short prayer or word that helps move them from the mental space of reasoning into another consciousness, the inward space where communion with God starts. It is for some as if we need to go through an inner door, and a brief word is the key to passing through the doorway.

The fundamental Quaker advice, enunciated many times by early Friends, was to stand still in the Light. We become aware of that dim inward light that illumines our inner darkness. When thoughts or fears or temptations intrude, the way is to use gentle persistence to hold our inward attention still. Do not allow the attention to roam, particularly do not deign to answer these intrusive thoughts, but subject them to the scrutiny of the Light. That is the meditative method. The key insight of Friends was to focus prayerful attention on the Light.

> *After thou seest thy thoughts and the temptations, do not think but submit; and then the Power comes. ... Stand still in the Light and submit to it, and the other will be hushed and gone; and then content comes. When temptations and troubles appear, sink*

down in that which is pure; and all will be hushed
and fly away.[90].

This Light is not the preserve of Quakers, it is universal (in all people). The Light is experienced by many of all faiths. For example, here are three quotes: one from the Hindu scripture the Bhagavad Gita, one from the Catholic monk Thomas Merton, and one from the ancient writings of Judaism:

> *Everything that is beautiful and good,*
> *whatever has power and glory*
> *is only a portion of my own radiance.*[91]

> *The Christian way of perfection is then in every*
> *sense a way of love, of gratitude, of trust in God.*
> *Nowhere do we depend on our own strength or on*
> *our own light: our eyes are fixed on Christ who*
> *gives all light and strength...*[92]

> *The sun shall be no more thy light by day; neither*
> *for brightness shall the moon give light unto thee;*
> *but the Lord shall be unto thee an everlasting light,*
> *and thy God thy glory. (Isaiah 61:19)*

None of these quotes means that Quaker prayer is much the same as Hindu or Catholic or Hebrew prayer, neither do they mean that Quaker prayer life is any better or worse. They are all ways to approach God, and many people find the use of devotional readings from other faiths very helpful. The Quaker prayer life, as I have described it, has the same aim as other faiths, some of the same pattern of practice, and it differs primarily in its emphasis on silent worship as the primary spiritual testimony. We hold that testimony most dear and find by experience it is the most effective method of prayer. The Quaker practice was to turn the inward attention to the Light, however dim, ignoring all else, mentally turning our "back on the world" and then to "keep low". The Quaker experience is that it is in this total, pure, inward silence that the disparate parts of ourselves become unified.

Beyond the Divided Self

Early Friends also recognised, and it is especially clear in the
writings of Fox, Nayler, Crisp and Penington, that we each
have two voices within us. For some time, maybe months, our
prayer time will be dominated by the voice of the world, the
Self, and we need to wait patiently for this voice to start to be
silenced. Then we can start to hear the other voice, the quiet
voice of the Spirit. Our role in that inward silence is to
distinguish these and to favour the second [my emphasis in
bold text][93]

> *And I found there were two thirsts in me, the one
> after the creatures, to have gotten help and strength
> there, and the other after the Lord and creator and
> his Son Jesus Christ. And I saw all the world could
> do me no good. ...And I saw professors, priests, and
> people were whole and at ease in that condition
> which was my misery, and they loved that which I
> would have been rid of.[94]*

> *And as many as honestly desire to be heirs of this
> holy power and kingdom, patiently wait till you feel
> that move in you which is of that pure nature, and
> having felt it alive in you, rejoice in it with hope and
> faith, and keep therein, and be not discouraged,
> because of the littleness of it in your present sight,
> neither do you judge and measure it thereby; for you
> know not what power it has with God, and how
> precious it is in His sight; and what it will obtain for
> you at His hands in the time of need, you have not
> yet proved, nor can you, while you have things
> greater in your thoughts than it to run to: The power
> of holiness and truth in the inward parts is not
> known but in the depth, when the fire of wrath comes
> upon all vain hopes and hypocritical confidence,
> when all that is without a man is removed far away;
> when all friends and acquaintance are become
> farther off than strangers, and whatever thing the*

*creature seeks to for comfort, turns against him, and adds to his grief; then is known the power of holiness and truth in heart with God, and a clean conscience will speak peace; and none can take it away from you, if you abide but in it: He that has proved it commends it to you, who has been stripped of all, that you might learn and know the treasure of life, and holiness with God. **Wherefore judge not that which is holier and lower than yourselves, but let that which is just and holy, judge that which is above it in you, which is not of that nature...***

So you must not fix your faith on that which seems strong and great in you, because it is so, nor because it is likely, nor because it promises great things; but believe in that which is most holy, true and just in you, that to the Anointing of the most Holy you may come in your particular, and He will bring you into the assembly of the Sanctified, where the Holy One reigns over all....

*And all the world take notice of this, wherever it comes; this is He whom the Father of lights has now sent into you that are in the world, the Holy One of God, sent to call you and give you light, who says, I am the light of the world: hear Him, and believe, that you may become children of light and truth. This is the glad tidings and Gospel of Jesus Christ, who is preached to you in the world. Professions and forms, would limit the Holy One to themselves, and exclude others; but God's gift is free in Christ Jesus, and His tender is to all men, who would have all men to be saved, and come to the knowledge of the truth; none He excludes, but who will not receive His gift, His Son, the most Holy which calls you, who through the preaching of the Gospel is come near you; yea, **He is in you with His light, giving you to see the way out of darkness, which no other could do for you;** and without money or price you* *have Him: If you receive Him, and keep His sayings, and obey His movings, He will dwell in you, and take up His abode, and you shall know that the Father has sent Him to call you out of the world into the light of life.[95]*

In a similar vein Isaac Penington answers the question: "If the true faith does not come from practices, duties and ordinances of established church behaviours, where does this true faith come from?"

It is that power of believing which springs out of the seed of eternal life; and leavens the heart, not with notions of knowledge, but with the powers of life. The other faith is drawn out of man's nature, by considerations which affect the natural part, and is kept alive by natural exercises of reading, hearing, praying studying, meditating in that part; but this springs out of the seed of life given, and grows up in the life of that seed...[96]

As Nayler noted above, the key is to allow that lower, deeply felt, at first minimal presence to be the guide and judge of all else; that is, do not allow the worldly assessment to judge whether the seed of life is up to scratch or not!

The fiery young early Quaker preacher James Parnell was well aware that the Light and its promptings and voice are to be followed, and that the alternative inner voice of doubt and discouragement is not:

And although we are kept in prison, yet it is for the Lord's appointed time; therefore, Friends, eye the Lord in all these things, and look not out at man, nor at what man can do, either for or against us; but eye God in all his works and in all his instruments, and there will be no cause for discouragement; for discouragement and fears, doubts and questionings, spring from the carnal mind.[97]

Early Quakers felt the life arise within them very slowly at first, and each had to pay very careful committed attention to the little stirring within. Our worldly, or earthly, selves will try to re-assert their commentary and explanations of our inner world, but the advice is to resist this easy way out, and to stay very low within, very humble, and wait for the faint stirrings of the divine life to appear. Isaac Penington noted:

> *It not an easy matter, in all cases, clearly and understandingly to discern the voice of the Shepherd, the motions of God's Spirit, and certainly to distinguish the measure of life from all other voices, motions and appearances whatsoever. Through much growth in the truth, through much waiting on the Lord, through much fear and trembling, through much sobriety and meekness, through much exercise of the senses, this is at last given and obtained.[98]*

Any self-comforting thought that we are beginning to understand what God is about should be resisted, any thoughts of gratitude should be embraced. This rarely happens in one sitting! Both George Fox and Isaac Penington, for example, had some very clear instructions about this first stirring of the Life within.

> *[K]eep thy mind low, up to the Lord God; and deny thyself. And from thy own will, that is, the earthly, thou must be kept. Then thou wilt feel the power of God....[99]*

> *For though I had a true taste of life and power from God; yet not knowing the foundation there could be no true building with it; and so the spirit was quenched. ...But at length it pleased life to move in a low way in the midst of the powers of darkness in my heart; and by sinking low out of the wisdom, out of the reason, out of all high imaginations, and trusting*

myself to it; though dreadful strokes and oppositions were felt from the powers of darkness, yet at length there as some appearance of the deliverer...

When God begets life in the heart, there is the savour of it in they vessel, and a secret, living warmth and virtue, which the heart in some measure feels, whereby it is known. Lie low in the fear of the Most High, that this leaven may grow and increase in thee.[100]

The Life is renewed every day. This Life is not something we feel and then we can assume is there for good; and it is a great mistake to then transfer that feeling ourselves to everything we see and do. It is not like a piece of worldly knowledge we acquire and then can use at will. Instead we are to depend on a fresh gift of the Spirit in every event of every day. This is why the daily practice of morning prayer is so important, for it is the way to be provided with "daily bread" as food for the soul.

Know in what light it is to walk, which is in the light of the spirit ... [which] shineth fresh in the renewed spirit every day, and so is gathering it more and more inward into itself, comprehending it in itself, and preserving it in its own purity, clearness and brightness... seeing a necessity of depending on the Spirit for fresh light and life every day to every spiritual motion.[101]

If we lose that sense and feeling of the presence of the Life of the Spirit, we cannot regain it by rituals or repeating what happened before. The only way is to wait patiently, in prayer, without words:

When the life at any time is lost, the only way of recovery is by retiring to the invisible, and keeping there, and growing up there; and not coming forth in the visible further than the life leads, nor staying there longer than the life stays.[102]

The Quaker method in prayer then was not just the emptying of the whole by endless meditation, nor was it just a quiet personal prayer time with God using well-known prayers from the church liturgy. The real power came from an emptying, and a patient waiting for the first, faint stirrings of the presence within, in a most mysterious way, and then from a committed attention to the inward motions. It took committed attention, an attitude of inward humility and keeping low, an intent to favour and focus on these faint stirrings of the Light rather than to give weight to worldly thoughts and assessments. This process took a careful discernment that came with practice.

The evidence is that this faint measure began to grow within them as they began to obey the requirements of the Light, and became the source of the power and transformation in their lives. They were changed men and women.

> *Friends, whose Minds are turn'd to the Light, which comes from Jesus Christ, which never changeth, whose Light enlightens everyone coming into the World; in it abide, and in it walk, and to it be faithful and obedient in your Measures, that with it your Minds may be guided up to God, who is the Father of Lights, that you may bring your Deeds to the Light, to try whether they are wrought in God.*[103]

All this may sound terribly complicated, and indeed there are many layers in prayer. However the basic Quaker attitude in prayer is very, very simple. It is this. We are not very good at resolving all the conflicting issues in our lives. The continuing inner wrestling of competing thoughts and possible paths is very wearing. So we inwardly acknowledge our inabilities and openly ask the Inward Light to show us what to do, listening carefully and paying close attention and following the promptings and intimations for action we are given. The Light, the working of God within us, knows MUCH better than we do. Then we are on the way to peace.

Encouragement and Perseverance

The developing of a deep and intimate relationship with the divine Light, with God, with Jesus, or whichever terms are meaningful to you, requires serious effort, perseverance, faith and hope. The writings of early Friends attested the lengthy cleansing and spiritual healing which had to occur: remember that Fox had made a single-minded spiritual pursuit for nine years before he fully understood his mission in life on Pendle Hill in 1652.

Sarah Jones gives tender encouragement, based on her own experience, for all to continue with daily prayer (inward retirement), despite the intruding thoughts (from the gadding, hunting Esau):

> *So cease thy mourning, thou weeping babe, that mourns in secret for manifestations from thy beloved, as thou hast had in dayes past; for I can testifie unto thee by experience, whosoever thou art in that state, that he is bringing thee nearer to him, for that was but milk which he fed thee when thou was weak, but he will feed thee with the Word from whence that milk proceedeth, if thou be willing and obedient to live at home with Jacob, which is to daily retire thy mind; though the gadding, hunting Esau persecutes thee for it, thou shalt receive the blessing in which all happiness and felicity doth consist for evermore.*[104]

Edward Burrough, after faithfully following the Inward Guide, described in his last hours in February 1663 to Francis Howgill, the wonderful divine gift he had received:

> *Now my soul and spirit is centred in to its own being with God,...*[105]

Here is encouragement from *The Cloud of Unknowing*:

So go on, I beg you, with all speed. Look forward, not backward. See what you lack, not what you have already; for that is the quickest way of getting and keeping humility. Your whole life now must be one of longing, if you are to achieve perfection. And this longing must be in the depths of your will, put there by God...[106]

The modern Quaker Thomas Kelly put it this way:

How, then, shall we lay hold of that Life and Power, and live the life of prayer without ceasing? By quiet, persistent practice in turning of all our being, day and night, in prayer and inward surrender, ... Lapses and forgettings are so frequent. Our surroundings grow so exciting. But when you catch yourself again, lose no time in self-recriminations, but breathe a silent prayer for forgiveness and begin again, just where you are.[107]

To you ... who are seekers, to you, young and old who have toiled all night and found nothing, but who want to launch out into the deeps and let down your nets for a draught, I want to speak, as simply, as tenderly, as clearly as I can. For God can be found. ...There is a Divine Center into which all your life can slip. A new and absolute orientation to God, a Center where you can live with Him, and out of which you see all of life, through new and radiant vision tinged with new sorrows and pangs, new joys unspeakable and full of glory.[108]

In Summary

Quaker prayer arises from a life of continuing devotion.[109] We learn by experience.

The first step is a daily and continuing practice to centre down, turning to the inward light no matter how dim at first, and cultivating an inward listening. Disregard the intrusions of thoughts, however plausible, which commonly appear as mental reasonings and justifications, even if apparently disguised as "higher thoughts". These intrusions can be briefly examined and will be seen invariably to be manifestations of the Self or Ego. They arise from pride or vainglory which is an intellectual satisfaction of knowing "what's what," or from worldly desires such as gluttony, lust or avarice, or from fear of losing worldly possessions, which is avarice in disguise, or from spiritual torpor or laziness—in other words the "seven sins". "Stand still in the Light" inwardly refusing to be diverted. Submit everything to the scrutiny of the inward Light; sink low and allow the Light to judge and dispel these illusory thoughts from the Self.

The second step is a mental willingness and desire to be free of all the imaginations and workings of the mind so that the entire being is directed inwardly to God. This inward yielding is an act of humble submission, and an acknowledgment that all is in God's hands and in God's time. We admit our dependence on God. The sanctification or purifying of the heart and soul is done in the inner darkness, unknown and unfelt by us at the time. That is why we must learn to reside in that inner darkness without expecting wonderful spiritual delights and consolations every time we spare time for prayer. Coming wholeheartedly to the act of prayer is more important than the results of the prayer.

The third step is to love the Light as it begins to show us what to do and what needs to be remedied in our lives to make us more acceptable in God's sight. Some of these instructions will seem unacceptable or daunting at first. We need to give priority to the small voice or dim light within us and allow that to judge what is more worldly. We must reverse the usual behaviour of allowing our mind to judge the small, divine seed hidden beneath this veil of worldly commentary. We must "keep low" within ourselves. In the early Quaker language, we must crucify this opposition of the Self to God's working within us. We are to follow Jesus teachings. Fox's words were: *"I brought them under Christ's teaching, or to sit at the feet of their teacher Jesus".*[110]

Prayer is a conscious choice to seek God. The attentiveness, waiting in silent prayer, is practice for listening to God during the rest of the day. The difficulties we experience in inward prayer are preparation for our outward lives, for each time we return to the centre in prayer we are modelling how to live our lives; each time we dismiss the internal intrusions we are strengthening that of God within us and denying the role of the Self; every time we turn to prayer and to God we are seeking to increase the measure of Light in our lives. The end result is the old Self dies and a new being emerges, in a new "wineskin".

So the prime attitude in Quaker prayer is very simple: Truth, the inward guide, unchanging and ever-reliable, will show us how to live and integrate our lives, and will bring us closer to God.

It is clear that this inward yielding and obedience to the Light was the source of the extraordinary connectedness with God experienced by the early Quakers. It is also the source of their inspiration, inward clarity, steadfastness and courage that "turned the world upside down".

ACKNOWLEDGEMENTS

I have been greatly encouraged by Helen Gould, and helped by many people in coming to this understanding of Quaker prayer. Gerard Guiton sent me copies of various pertinent early Quaker pamphlets whenever I posed a question. Hugh Barbour read an earlier draft and pointed out several improvements. Alice Sowall has also helped clarify the wordings and editing style. Charles Martin has been a perceptive editor, provided very helpful clarifications and also drew my attention to the quote from Francis Howgill on page 44.

David Johnson is a Member of Queensland Regional Meeting of the Australia Yearly Meeting of the Religious Society of Friends. David is a geologist with both industry and academic experience, and wrote *The Geology of Australia*, specifically for the general public. He has a long commitment to nonviolence and opposing war and the arms trade, and has worked with the International Campaign to Ban Landmines. David delivered the 2005 Backhouse Lecture to Australia Yearly Meeting on *Peace is a Struggle*. He was part of the work to establish the Silver Wattle Quaker Centre in Australia in 2010, and is Co-Director of the Centre for 2013-14.

Appendix - Techniques That Some Have Found Helpful

The inner silence, the way it comes and goes, is beyond our control. However we can still work towards it. How might we start and assist this process? Many people need a key to pass though the door to prayer.[111] For some, just a humble lifting of the heart to God is all that it takes.

The original Quaker way was to hold oneself inwardly still in the Light no matter how faint that Light, and return to it whenever we become aware of the wanderings of the mind. Concentrate on that stillness, in the same way that breathing meditation concentrates and returns to the breath. When the Spirit is strongly present with us, there is little need to follow set routines. However, at the beginning and in times of trouble, a practised process can be very helpful. Here are a few, and the Spirit will guide you. My own experience is the Spirit will vary the instruction.

Many find the meditation technique of following your breathing is a very good way to start, and attending a meditation retreat for a weekend or a week can be a very good way to develop this skill and find your way inwards. Attention to the breathing also grounds us in the present, the "now,"[112] and restrains us from worrying or dreaming about the past or the future. While this method is now associated primarily with the eastern religions of Buddhism and Hinduism, my own readings convince me it was a regular practice for early Christians as well.

At times when the mind tends to wander immediately it can be helpful to open the eyes and spend five minutes concentrating your attention on an object within your field of view, perhaps a single flower, or the edge of a patterned chair or the corner of a picture. Take time to return your gaze to this and hold it in your attention exclusive of all else. Practise an attentive awareness of it without allowing descriptive or related thoughts into your mind. It is hard to meditate if the mind cannot concentrate. When your concentration is more steady close your eyes and resume meditation. Try to turn your awareness to your heart and diaphragm—away from your head.

Many people find a short memorised prayer stabilises their time in prayer—the Lord's Prayer or some verses from one of the psalms. This technique is really just going back for a while into an earlier relationship with God. The desert fathers used the first lines from Psalm 70: *"O God come to my assistance, O Lord make haste to help me"*. These words expressed the complete submission and trust and reliance on God that is necessary for true prayer.

The eastern Orthodox Christians found the Jesus prayer most helpful, saying and then mouthing *"Lord Jesus Christ have mercy on me"*, repeated continually, and then in rhythm with the heartbeat or breathing. Eventually this prayer may begin to recite itself, to pray, from the heart.

The technique of Centring Prayer advises each prayer session start with an acknowledgment and plea for God to be present during this time. Then take a word or image that the Spirit provides and use this, rolling it over inwardly whenever you discover your mind has wandered.[113] Some find a short mantra helpful.[114] Most writers advise to choose just a single word,[115] which is breathed inwardly, repeatedly if needed until the inner attention is stabilised at our centre. Longer phrases or thoughts easily engage the mind and the imagination, and before we know it our attention was wandered widely. In earlier times I used a word that the Spirit had emplaced unexpectedly in my consciousness, like 'commitment', 'dishonesty', and 'trust'. I was led to use for a while the "I am", the puzzling and for some the most difficult words in scripture.[116]

Another method is to focus our attention on the intruding words, just look at them. Magically they may disappear, as if they have suddenly been exposed, are embarrassed and cannot stand to be watched. An internal instruction to me was to say internally, "I will neither pay you attention nor not pay you attention".

Each of us must find the most helpful method. And many people practise one of them to maintain an inner attentiveness in a busy world, or return to one of them in times of difficulty. Yet these techniques have a downside, since each also imposes a subtle barrier between you and the deep emptiness and awareness of God we seek. That is the attraction of the Quaker advice of standing still in the Light and holding yourself silently aware and ready for the Spirit, for this process works on becoming still and empty without asking the mind to keep doing something till we get there.

End Notes

[1] Also reprinted in *Journal of George Fox*, (Nickalls edition), 1975, p. xliv.

[2] Clifton Wolters (translator), 1985. *The Cloud of Unknowing and Other Works.* Penguin 232pp. See p. 98.

[3] Gerard Guiton, 2012. *The Early Quakers and the 'Kingdom of God'.* Inner Light Books 506pp.

[4] Douglas Gwyn, 1995. *The Covenant Crucified: Quakers and the Rise of Capitalism.* Pendle Hill Publications, Wallingford PA. 403pp.

[5] C.H. Dodd, 1953. The Interpretation of the Fourth Gospel. Cambridge University Press, 478pp. See p. 87.

[6] *Journal of George Fox*, (Nickalls edition, 1975), p.8.

[7] Elizabeth Bathurst 1679, An EPISTLE To You five in particular, *viz.* A.W. E.T. M.J. B.P. & E.F. unto whom this is more especially to be Delivered, p.87. Reproduced in Mary Garman, Judith Applegate, Margaret Benefiel & Dortha Meredith (editors), 1996. *Hidden In Plain Sight: Quaker Women's Writings 1650-1700.* Pendle Hill Publications, Wallingford PA. p. 387.

[8] D.W Lambert, 1906. *The Quiet in the Land: Some Quaker Saints Challenge Us Today.* The Epworth Press.101pp. See p.74.

[9] Edward Burrough, Epistle to the reader, prefixed in Fox's *Great Misterey.* Quoted by W.C. Braithwaite, 1912. *The Beginnings of Quakerism*, p. 130.

[10] D.W. Lambert, 1906. *The Quiet in the Land: Some Quaker Saints Challenge Us Today.* The Epworth Press.101pp. See p. 96.

[11] D.W. Lambert, 1906. *The Quiet in the Land: Some Quaker Saints Challenge Us Today.* The Epworth Press.101pp. See p.86. The last words are from Psalm 72:26.

[12] John d'Emilio, 2003. *Lost Prophet The Life and Times of Bayard Rustin*. Free Press, p. 26.

[13] Clifton Wolters (translator), 1985. *The Cloud of Unknowing and Other Works*. Penguin 232pp. See p. 63.

[14] Thomas Kelly, 1988. *Have You Ever Seen a Miracle?* p.143-161 in *The Eternal Promise*. Second edition. Friends United Press, Richmond, Indiana. 165pp.

[15] Jesus' habit of spending time alone in prayer, commonly up on a mountain, is mentioned elsewhere in the gospels, e.g. Mark 1:35-36, 6:45-46; Luke 4:1-14, 5:16; John 6:15, 8:1-2.

[16] 1Thessalonians 5: 17.

[17] Elizabeth Bathurst 1679, *An EPISTLE* To You five in particular, *viz.* A.W. E.T. M.J. B.P. & E.F. unto whom this is more especially to be Delivered, p.128. Reproduced in Mary Garman, Judith Applegate, Margaret Benefiel & Dortha Meredith (editors), 1996. *Hidden In Plain Sight: Quaker Women's Writings 1650-1700*. Pendle Hill Publications, Wallingford PA. p. 403.

[18] Helen Gould, 2009. *The Quaking Meeting*. The Backhouse Lecture 2009. Religious Society of Friends (Quakers) in Australia. 69pp.

[19] Brother Lawrence, *The Practice of the Presence of God*. Mowbray 1980, p.25.

[20] Alexander Parker, convinced in 1653, wrote these words as part of a Letter to Friends dated 14 xi 1659 (14/1/1660), printed in Thomas Salthouse and Alexander Parker, *A manifestation of divine love...*,1660, p.15-17; reprinted in Abram Rawlinson Barclay, ed., *Letters &c of early friends*, 1841, pp. 365-6. The extract in the British Quaker Faith & Practice 2.41 omits the words "be not careless ...in some place and".

[21] George Fox, 1652. Epistle 19. Also in *Truth of the Heart*, p.12. Fox makes this claim in the Journal, e.g. p. 74, 171, 203, 214. Fox and the early Friends ceased to revere church buildings, calling them "steeplehouses," noting that each person is a temple of God, rather

than the places of bricks and mortar, a teaching justified by the scripture: Acts 7:48, 17:24-27; 1 Corinthians 3:16, 6:19. For Friends, the church is the community of believers, not the building.

[22] The words 'feel' and 'find' are from Acts 17: 27, in a sermon from Paul which describes an inward spirituality very much as also practised by the early Quakers.

[23] Sarah Jones, 1650. *This Lights appearance in the Truth to all precious dear Lambs of the Life, Dark vanished, Light shines forth: Set forth*, p.3. Reproduced in Mary Garman, Judith Applegate, Margaret Benefiel & Dortha Meredith (editors), 1996. *Hidden In Plain Sight: Quaker Women's Writings 1650-1700*. Pendle Hill Publications, Wallingford PA. p. 35.

[24] Isaac Penington, 1671. *Some directions to the panting soul*. This extract also in *Quaker Faith and Practice*, The Religious Society of Friends (Quakers) in Britain 1999, # 26.70.

[25] Many writers record their own experience that much work had to be done early in the process and then God began to assist and prayer became easier (see, for example, writings by Brother Lawrence and Teresa of Avila).

[26] Rex Ambler, 2008. *Light to Live By*. Quaker Books. 60pp.

[27] George Fox, 1653. Epistle 35, also quoted in Rex Ambler (2001) *Truth of The Heart*, p.22.

[28] John Bellers, 1718. An Epistle to the Quarterly-meeting of London and Middlesex. 15pp. Quoted in W.C. Braithwaite, 1919. *The Second Period of Quakerism*, p. 575. Macmillan and Co., London,

[29] Roger Hebden, 1655. Letter, quoted on p.252 by Gerard Guiton *The Early Quakers and the 'Kingdom of God'*, 2012. Inner Light Books, 506pp.

[30] George Fox, 1658. Letter to Lady Claypole, quoted in *Journal of George Fox*, (Nickalls edition, 1975), p.346-348.

[31] William Shewen, 1683. COUNSEL to the CHRISTIAN-TRAVELLER: Also MEDITATIONS & EXPERIENCES. Reprinted by Inner Light Books, San Francisco, California. 2008, 116pp. See p.97-98.

[32] H.H. Brinton, 1972. *Quaker Journals*. Pendle Hill Publications. 129pp, pp 28. George Whitehead, 1725 *The Christian Progress of That Ancient Servant and Minister of Jesus Christ, George Whitehead …*,

[33] The Epistle of Privy Counsel has similar advice: "… do not worry about the next step, but just stop thinking your 'good' thoughts as well as your 'bad' ones. … Let him [God] be himself, please, and nothing else. You are not to go probing into him with your smart and subtle ideas". Clifton Wolters (translator), 1985. *The Cloud of Unknowing and Other Works.* Penguin 232pp. See p.161.

[34] Closing paragraph added to *An Epistle to the Quarterly meeting of London and Middlesex*, printed in 1718. Quoted in W.C. Braithwaite, 1919. *The Second Period of Quakerism*, p. 576. Macmillan and Co., London.

[35] Brother Lawrence had a similar view: *"That useless thoughts spoil all; that the mischief began there, but that we ought to reject them as soon as we perceived their impertinence to the matter in hand or our salvation, and return to our communion with God"* from *The Practice of the Presence of God*, Mowbray 1980, p.9.

[36] Helena Wong, 2003. *"a door opens"* , p.108 in *Decent Exposure by 6 Journey Women*. Mountain Wildfire Press. 209pp.

[37] Isaac Penington, 1663. *Concerning God's Seeking out His Israel* II.395-6, quoted in *Knowing the Mystery of the Life Within* by R. Melvin Keiser & Rosemary Moore. Quaker Books 2005, p.155-6.

[38] Saint Augustine, 1961. *The Confessions*, translated by R.S. Pine-Coffin. Penguin Books, p.87.

[39] Stephen Crisp, 1694. *A Journal of the Life of Stephen Crisp.* Reproduced in Barbour, H. and Roberts, A.O., 2004. *Early Quaker Writings 1659-1700.* Pendle Hill Publications, p.205-6.

---

[40] James Nayler, 1660. Collection 1716, p.661.

[41] Gerard Hughes, 1985. *God of Surprises*. Darton, Longman & Todd, p.119.

[42] *Journal of George Fox* (Nickalls Edition, 1975) p.15.

[43] 2 Corinthians , 11: 13-14.

[44] Martha Paxton Grundy, 1999. *Tall Poppies Supporting the Gifts of Ministry and Eldering in the Monthly Meeting.*   Pendle Hill Pamphlet 347, p.5.

[45] The same message was articulated by Fox many times. E.g. In his 1653 tract *To all that would know the way to the Kingdom*, an extract of which is quoted in Rex Ambler, 2002. *Light to Live By*. Quaker Books, p.8-9. Also see the Journal (Nickalls edition) p.234-235.

[46] Elizabeth Gray Vining, 1959. *Friend of Life*. Michael; Joseph London. 350pp. See pp.47-48.

[47] The same advice is given by James Nayler (originally dated 1659, reproduced in Quaker Faith & Practice, 1999, 21.65): "*Art thou in the darkness? Mind it not, for if thou dost it will fill thee more, but stand still and act not, and wait in patience till Light arises out of Darkness to lead thee*".

[48] There are abundant examples of this attitude in the writings of early Quakers. The quote is Luke Cock in a sermon at York in 1721 (Quaker Faith & Practice, 1999, 20.22).

[49] See discussion and quotes in Martha Paxton Grundy, 1999. *Tall Poppies Supporting the Gifts of Ministry and Eldering in the Monthly Meeting.*   Pendle Hill Pamphlet 347, p.3-4.

[50] John Lampen, 1981. *Wait in the Light. The Spirituality of George Fox*. Quaker Home Service, 118pp. See especially p.79-92.

[51] *Journal of George Fox*, (Nickalls edition, 1975), p. 12-13.

[52] George Fox, 1706. *Gospel Truth Demonstrated.*

[53] William Smith, 1663. *A Manifestation of Prayer in Formality, and Prayer in the Spirit of God.*

[54] This is an ancient Hebrew and Christian spiritual understanding, e.g., Psalms 25:4-5, 86:11, 143:10. St Bonaventure (1221-1274) wrote at the start of his treatise *On the Perfection of Life Addressed to Sisters:* "Happy the man whom you instruct, O Lord, whom by your law you teach [Ps 93:12]. No one, admittedly, is to be esteemed wise save only him who is taught by the unction of the Spirit". *The Works of Bonaventure I Mystical Opuscula.* St Anthony Guild Press 1960, p.209. Similarly, the fourteenth-century *Epistle of Privy Counsel* (Chapter 12) is clear: "*However it is quite certain one cannot taste or experience God spiritually except by grace, whatever the extent of knowledge, acquired or natural. Therefore I beg you seek experience rather than knowledge: knowledge can often lead one astray through pride, whereas humble, loving experience does not lie*". Clifton Wolters (translator), 1985. *The Cloud of Unknowing and Other Works*, p.98-199. Penguin 232pp. Also note 1 Corinthians 8:1.

[55] William Penn, 1668. *No Cross, No Crown.* Chapter V, Sections 3 and 6. This was originally written in 1668 during Penn's imprisonment in the Tower of London and enlarged later and reprinted many times. This quote from Penn also reminds us of the comments in James 4:3, "*Ye ask, and receive not, because ye ask amiss, that ye may consume it upon your lusts*".

[56] William Penn, 1668. *No Cross, No Crown* II.6

[57] W.C. Braithwaite, 1919. *The Second Period of Quakerism*, p. 573-574. Macmillan and Co., London.

[58] Jeremiah (18:1-6) records his experience of a prompting and the resulting realisation that we are each in God's hands and that divine work is possible within our hearts to gradually change and perfect us.

[59] The human tendency to take credit for the workings of God within us as well as for the blessings of our life has been a stumbling block for all to deal with. See also Deuteronomy 8:1-20, Job Chapters 38-

41; Isaiah 55: 8-11. Jesus phrased our dependency on God in more positive terms: Matthew 6: 25-34.

[60] Stephen Crisp, 1694. *A Journal of the Life of Stephen Crisp.* Reproduced in Barbour, H. and Roberts, A.O., 2004. *Early Quaker Writings 1659-1700.* Pendle Hill Publications, p.204. A similar spiritual admission was made by George Fox in 1647, see the Journal p.14: '*And the Lord opened me that I saw through all these troubles and temptations*'.

[61] Isaac Penington, letter to Widow Walmsley etc, 24 July 1679. Reproduced p.114 in R. Melvin Kreiser & Rosemary Moore, 2005. *Knowing the Mystery of Life Within, Selected Writings of Isaac Penington in Their Historical and Theological Context.* Quaker Books, 322pp.

[62] Sandra Cronk, 1991. *Dark Night Journey: Inward Re-patterning Toward a Life Centred in God.* Pendle Hill Publications, Wallingford PA. 179pp. See pp.45-56.

[63] Rex Ambler, 2008. *Light to Live By.* Quaker Books. 60pp. See p.47.

[64] See *Journal of George Fox*, (Nickalls edition, 1975), p. 14-15.

[65] Another ancient understanding repeated by the New Testament apostles—see Isaiah 64:4 and Jeremiah 9:24.

[66] 1 Corinthians 2: 6-11 (NIV)

[67] *The Works of Bonaventure I Mystical Opuscula. On the Perfection of Life, Addressed to Sisters.* St Anthony Guild Press 1960, p. 212, 215.

[68] Robert Barclay, as quoted in *Quaker Classics in Brief*, Pendle Hill Publications1978, p.62. Also published as *Barclay in Brief, An Abbreviation of Robert Barclay's Apology for the True Christian Divinity* by Eleanor Price Mather, 1942. Pendle Hill Pamphlet 28.

[69] See also 1 Samuel 15:22.

[70] William Smith, 1663. *A Manifestation of Prayer in Formality, and Prayer in the Spirit of God,* p.1.

[71] *Journal of George Fox* (Nickalls Edition, 1975), for example see pp. 167, 176, 232, 288, 292.

[72] For example: "It is a Principle of Divine Light and Life of Christ Jesus, placed in the Conscience, which opens the Understanding, enlightens the Eyes of the Mind…" from Elizabeth Bathurst 1695, *An EPISTLE* To You five in particular, *viz.* A.W. E.T. M.J. B.P. & E.F. unto whom this is more especially to be Delivered. Part II Concerning the Principle of Truth. Reproduced in Mary Garman, Judith Applegate, Margaret Benefiel & Dortha Meredith (editors), 1996. *Hidden In Plain Sight: Quaker Women's Writings 1650-1700,* Pendle Hill Publications, Wallingford PA, p. 381.

[73] *Journal of George Fox* (Nickalls Edition, 1975), for example see pp. 155, 294, 339.

[74] From Francis Howgill's Testimony Concerning Edward Burrough, in *The memorable works of a son of thunder and consolation namely that true prophet and faithful servant of God and sufferer for the testimony of Jesus, Edward Burroughs, who dyed a prisoner for the word of God in the city of London, the fourteenth of the twelfth moneth, 1662.* Printed and published for the good and benefit of generations to come ..., 1672.

[75] The Quaker experience was that each person is given a measure of the Light, of faith, of connectedness with God (Romans 12:3, Ephesians 4:7), and that our measure can be increased by following the Light. We are not to boast or go beyond our measure (Romans 12:3, 2 Corinthians 10:13,15 and 2 Corinthians 12:7). Careful discernment is required to know our own measure, and to live obediently within that measure. In comparison, Jesus was accorded fullness not just a measure (Luke 4:1, John1:14, John 3:34, Colossians 1:19).

[76] Sarah Jones, 1650. *This Lights appearance in the Truth to all precious dear Lambs of the Life, Dark vanished, Light shines forth: Set forth.* Reproduced in Mary Garman, Judith Applegate, Margaret Benefiel & Dortha Meredith (editors), 1996. *Hidden In Plain Sight:*

Quaker Women's Writings 1650-1700, Pendle Hill Publications, Wallingford PA p. 35.

[77] William Dewsbury, 1655. *A True Prophecy of the Mighty Day of the Lord.* Reproduced in Barbour, H. and Roberts, A.O., 2004. *Early Quaker Writings 1659-1700.* Pendle Hill Publications, p.100.

[78] William Shewen, 1683. COUNSEL to the CHRISTIAN-TRAVELLER: Also MEDITATIONS & EXPERIENCES. Reprinted by Inner Light Books, San Francisco, California. 2008, 116pp. See p. 95.

[79] See for example *Journal of George Fox*, (Nickalls edition, 1975), pp. 231, 232, 235, 288, 292, 304, and also others listed below in Endnote 25.

[80] *Journal of George Fox* (Nickalls Edition, 1975) p.15. The section on pages 14-15 not only details his inner experience of these blocks between himself and God, but also that it is the Spirit working in his heart that showed him the false ways from the true waiting upon God.

[81] George Fox, 1654. *To all that would know the Way to the KINGDOME ... A Direction to turn your minds within, where the Voice of the true God is to be heard, whom you ignorantly worship as afarre off, and to wait upon him for the true Wisdom.* 13pp.

[82] James Parnell in Works, published 1675. See also 1 John 2:27. Quoted in *Daily Readings From Quaker Writings Ancient & Modern, Volume II,* edited by Linda Hill Renfer, 1995, p. 302, Serenity Press.

[83] Elizabeth Bathurst 1679, *An EPISTLE* To You five in particular, *viz.* A.W. E.T. M.J. B.P. & E.F. unto whom this is more especially to be Delivered, p.79. Reproduced in Mary Garman, Judith Applegate, Margaret Benefiel & Dortha Meredith (editors), 1996. *Hidden In Plain Sight: Quaker Women's Writings 1650-1700,* Pendle Hill Publications, Wallingford PA p. 384.

[84] The same instructions are given in *Journal of George Fox* (Nickalls Edition, 1975), p.117 from his time at Baycliff in 1652: *"their first step to peace—to stand still in the light that showed their*

sin and transgressions ... ". The same reaching is given many times in the Journal, e.g. pp. 176, 225-6, 232, 292, 303.

[85] *Journal of George Fox* (Nickalls Edition, 1975), p.12-13.

[86] William Penn, *No Cross, No Crown*, Chapters III. 1 and IV.2. Reprinted as abridged text in *Quaker Classics in Brief*, Pendle Hill Publications. 1978, p.7, 8, 9.

[87] Margaret Fell, 1656, *Living under the Light: An Epistle to Convinced Friends*. The abridged section quoted is from *Margaret Fell Speaking*, Pendle Hill Pamphlet 206 by Hugh Barbour 1976, p. 24.

[89] Thomas Ellwood, 1714. *Life*, pp.21-25. This need to focus on the inner thoughts as well as the outer behaviours avoids the common traps of saying and doing one thing outwardly while reserving an inner option to do otherwise. It reminds us of the primary teaching of the Buddha, the first verse of the Dhammapada —The Way of Life: "*Mind is the cause of all that we are; mind is the basis and they all are shaped by the mind. If one speaks or acts with an impure mind, then suffering follows one as the wagon wheel the hoof of the ox*".

[90] George Fox, 1652. Epistle 10.

[91] *The Bhagavad Gita*, Section 10:41-42, translated by Juan Mascaro (1962), p.51. Penguin Books. 86pp.

[92] Thomas Merton, 1964. *Life and Holiness*. Image Books, p.65.

[93] The same advice to ignore obvious thoughts and sensations and to focus on the more subtle, deeper movements is given in *The Cloud of Unknowing* (c. 1370): "*In this way you can see that we must concentrate our whole attention on this lowly movement of love in our will. To all other forms of sweetness or consolation, however pleasant or holy, we should show a sort of indifference. ... Therefore attend in humility to this unseeing movement of love in your heart*". Clifton Wolters (translator), 1985. *The Cloud of Unknowing*, p.120,121. Penguin 232 pp.

[94] *Journal of George Fox*, Nickalls edition, 1975, p. 12.

---

[95] James Nayler, 1659. *A Door Opened To The Imprisoned Seed.*

[96] Isaac Penington, 1659. *The Axe Laid to the Root of the Old Corrupt Tree*, quoted in *Knowing the Mystery of the Life Within* by R. Melvin Keiser & Rosemary Moore. Quaker Books 2005, p.187.

[97] James Parnell, reproduced in *Day By Day: Being a Compilation from the Writings of Ancient and Modern Friends.* Edited by William Crouch 1869. Wm. H. Chase, Dennis Bros. New York. p.186, and also in *Daily Readings From Quaker Writings Ancient & Modern*, edited by Linda Hill Renfer, 1988, p. 256, Serenity Press.

[98] Isaac Penington (ca.1665-1667), *Some Queries Concerning the Order and Government of the Church of Christ* II. 368-70, quoted in *Knowing the Mystery of the Life Within* by R. Melvin Keiser & Rosemary Moore. Quaker Books 2005, p.190.

[99] George Fox, 1658. Letter to Lady Claypole, quoted in *Journal of George Fox*, (Nickalls edition), 1975, p. 346-348.

[100] Isaac Penington, 1658. *The Way of Life and Death*, and Isaac Penington, 1661. *Some Directions to the Panting Soul*, both quoted in *Knowing the Mystery of the Life Within* by R. Melvin Keiser & Rosemary Moore. Quaker Books 2005, p.131 and p.141.

[101] Isaac Penington, 1661. *Some Directions to the Panting Soul*, quoted in *Knowing the Mystery of the Life Within* by R. Melvin Keiser & Rosemary Moore. Quaker Books 2005, p.141.

[102] Isaac Penington, 1659. *Babylon the Great Described*, quoted in *Knowing the Mystery of the Life Within* by R. Melvin Keiser & Rosemary Moore. Quaker Books 2005, p.139.

[103] An Epistle of M. Fell's to Friends, 1653, p.47. Reproduced in Mary Garman, Judith Applegate, Margaret Benefiel & Dortha Meredith (editors), 1996. *Hidden In Plain Sight: Quaker Women's Writings 1650-1700*, p. 452. This text is typical early Quaker writing, with a linking of several biblical texts: John 1:9, Romans 12:3, John 3:21, James 1:17.

[104] Sarah Jones, 1650. *This Lights appearance in the Truth to all precious dear Lambs of the Life, Dark vanished, Light shines forth: Set forth.* Reproduced in Mary Garman, Judith Applegate, Margaret Benefiel & Dortha Meredith (editors), 1996. *Hidden In Plain Sight: Quaker Women's Writings 1650-1700*, Pendle Hill Publications, Wallingford PA p. 36. See also Genesis 25:24-34; and 1 Corinthians 3:2, 1 Peter 2:2 for scriptural allusions.

[105] Howgill's Testimony. Quoted in W.C. Braithwaite, 1919. *The Second Period of Quakerism*, p. 27. Macmillan and Co., London.

[106] *The Cloud of Unknowing and Other Works*, 1985, Ch 2, p. 60, translated by Clifton Wolters, Penguin Books. 232pp.

[107] Thomas Kelly, 1941. *The Light Within.* In *A Testament of Devotion*, p.38-39. Harper & Row.

[108] Thomas Kelly, probably 1940. *Secret Seekers*, In *The Eternal Promise*, 1988, p.118. Friends United Press.

[109] Another recent example is in the writings of Herbert Hoover (1952) *Memoirs. Years of Adventure 1874-1920.* The Macmillan Company, 1952 pp.7-8. "*Individual Bible-reading was part of the Quaker concept of education—and before I left Iowa I had read the Bible in daily stints from cover to cover. Religious training among the Quakers in fact began almost from birth. Even the babies were present at the invariable family prayers and Bible readings every morning. They were taken to meeting every Sunday, since ... there was no other place in which to park them*".

[110] See for example *Journal of George Fox*, (Nickalls edition, 1975), pp. 107, 109, 111, 117, 208, 210, 213, 218, 307.

[111] Sheila Keane's Pendle Hill Pamphlet 339 *Prayer: Beginning Again* is a helpful summary.

[112] Eckhart Tolle, *The Power of Now.* New World Library, 1999, is a helpful book for many.

[113] E.g. Basil Pennington, 1980. *Centering Prayer. Renewing an Ancient Christian Prayer Form.* An Image Book, Doubleday. 254pp. See basic rules for centering prayer on p.65. Thomas

Keating, 1994. *Intimacy with God: An Introduction to Centering Prayer.*

[114] John Main, *Christian Meditation: Talks at Gethsemani* or *Moment of Christ.* Father Main recommended using the prayer-phrase *Maranatha,* which is Aramaic for "Come, Lord", as in I Corinthians 16: 22 and Revelation 22: 20.

[115] E.g. *The Cloud of Unknowing and Other Works,* 1985, translated by Clifton Wolters, Penguin Books. 232pp.

[116] The difference between the 'I' as the personal ego, and mystical 'I' of eternal divine presence is tackled by Joel Goldsmith (1981) in *The Mystical 'I'* (Mandala Books, Unwin paperbacks. 145pp.)